# VACATIONSCAPE
## DESIGNING TOURIST REGIONS

Second Edition

Clare A. Gunn, FASLA

**VNR** VAN NOSTRAND REINHOLD
——————New York

Printed in the United States of America
Designed by East End Graphic Arts

Van Nostrand Reinhold
115 Fifth Avenue
New York, New York 10003

Van Nostrand Reinhold International Company Limited
11 New Fetter Lane
London EC4P 4EE, England

Van Nostrand Reinhold
480 La Trobe Street
Melbourne, Victoria 3000, Australia

Nelson Canada
1120 Birchmount Road
Scarborough, Ontario, M1K 5G4, Canada

16 15 14 13 12 11 10 9 8 7 6 5 4 3 2

**Library of Congress Cataloging-in-Publication Data**
Gunn, Clare A.
   Vacationscape: the design of travel environments/
Clare A. Gunn.—2nd ed., rev.
      p.      cm.
   Bibliography: p.
   Includes index.
   ISBN 0-442-22679-9
   1. Tourist trade.   2. Recreation areas.
3. Architectural design.   4. Design.   I. Title
G155.A1G863   1988                            87-34614
333.7—dc19                                         CIP

# Contents

# Preface to Second Edition

Promptings for a revised edition of *Vacation-scape* came from two sources. Many changes in the field of tourism, some dramatic, have taken place since the first edition, sixteen years ago. Second, many of the concepts, principles, and observations regarding tourism are still valid and need repeating. Though iconoclastic at the time, the theme of compatibility between development and environmental protection, as described in the first edition, remains a potent challenge for tourism design and development.

Since the first edition tourism has continued to grow beyond all predictions and expectations. Not only do greater numbers of people travel, but they travel to more places and see and do more things. Before 1970 most tourist attractions were places with unusual or abundant natural resources. Now, man-made attractions—theme parks, casinos, race tracks, entertainment, shopping, souvenir and craft sales—are constituting a greater portion of total travel objectives. Not known until recently was the concept of market segmentation. A tourist was a tourist was a tourist. The current diversity of tourists places a new emphasis on the need for a variety of services, attractions, transportation, and promotion. Advanced technology, especially the use of computers in business operations and for research, has been felt throughout the tourism industry. Finally, the idea of tourism itself is being redefined. Formerly associated with pleasure travel, the term is becoming equated with *all* travel. Reflecting this transition are the many "travel-tourism" studies, organizations, and agencies that seek to define the meanings of and relationship between the two concepts. All these changes have stimulated much greater land development and raised many more issues of land design for tourism—further justification for a second edition.

At the same time, some things have not changed greatly over this sixteen-year span. In fact, several issues that were important in past decades are even more acute today. The proliferation of development—all development, not only tourism—has exacerbated many environmental concerns of the 1970s. This growth has also added to the complexity of policy interface among stakeholders, an issue that demands ever-greater networking. The viewpoint of travelers is yet to be fully understood by designers and developers of tourism. Today's travelers have many of the same problems as before, perhaps more. They must still learn about travel attractions and the best travel modes, and they continue to have ex-

# 1/

# Toward New Tourism Environments

The very foundation upon which all tourism rests is the land: soils, hills, valleys, ridges, mountains, streams, lakes, seas, and waterfronts. It is the difference between the lands at home and those at destinations that stimulates travel. Without attractions in destinations there would be no travel either for business or personal objectives. Yet tourism leaders throughout the world continue to be preoccupied with promotion, not with land or its design and development.

Consider a romantic sunset from the lanai of a honeymoon suite, a child's first step into sea foam, the first catch of fish, the delights of photographing wildlife, or the pleasures of hiking in a dense forest. By attending a business conference or visiting friends and relatives, as well as by undertaking a pleasure trip, the traveler is brought into a variety of interesting rural and urban land settings and developments. Even the special environments of air terminals, highways, and stream corridors leave indelible impressions on our minds as we travel. These and hundreds of other experiences are made possible by the design of the land base and the many developments on it.

Over the years, great increases in the volume and complexity of travel have dramatically changed our approach to tourism. Once thought to be entirely the result of promotion, tourism is now considered a major land-development issue. People are finally beginning to recognize that every piece of land used and enjoyed by tourists is owned by someone. This fact introduces thousands of separate land-use policies by all three major ownership sectors—commercial enterprise, nonprofit organizations, and governments.

The traveler is the only one who sees, uses, and experiences the collective tourism environment. Neither owners nor designers have his perspective. Yet, because this environment is the result of policies and decisions made by many landowners and managers, the great abundance and diversity of development now available to travelers is often offset by negative effects: visitor satisfaction—key to all tourism —is less than desired, businesses do not reach their full potential, and the land base suffers.

## IDEOLOGICAL INFLUENCES

One can understand the resulting environmental complexity better when it is examined with several key owner and developer ideologies in mind. Applied in a symbiotic manner, these ideologies can counterbalance one another productively. When carried to extremes,

Yellowstone Falls. (Photo courtesy National Park Service)

1

however, they cause conflict between polarized groups and impede the development of travel environments that meet all desired goals.

For example, the ideology of resource protection was spawned many years ago by environmentalists and advocated most strongly in the environment-conscious 1970s. Adherents abhor the uses to which industrious people, especially private landowners, put their land. Where tourism is concerned this means the fewer travelers the better, as they are perceived as destroyers of resources. "The future of tourism is paradoxical for tourists are destroying the very resources they came to enjoy. The same is often true of destinations promoting tourism."[1] Many organizations and agencies in the United States and elsewhere support this position.

At the opposite pole are those whose ideology centers on free enterprise and development. They believe that property is wealth and that the benefits of ownership are tied to the husbandry of that wealth. The development and pricing of products and services are sacred rights, not to be interfered with by environmentalists in or out of government. Those government agencies that actually develop and operate tourist facilities and services are seen as unfair competitors. The tourist business sector seldom realizes how dependent it is on natural and cultural resources. For example, many hoteliers and airlines, believing their products are solely rooms and seats, fail to recognize the value of surrounding attractions that bring travelers to their businesses.

Those who stress the significance of the nonprofit sector are of increasing importance for tourism, especially in the United States. They seek to fulfill broad social goals rather than obtain profits. Most of our historic sites, organization camps (for example, YMCA, YWCA, youth, and church camps), and outdoor theaters are owned and operated by nonprofit organizations. Because the ideology of preservation emphasizes the historic value of locations, attendant services needed by visitors are often given little regard.

Perhaps the most widely accepted ideology of tourism is that of promotion. The thesis is that by means of advertising, publicity, and public relations, any area can have tourism. Many states, provinces, and countries spend millions of dollars annually on promotion, proving that many tourism leaders have faith in the effectiveness of such expenditures. There is evidence that some promotion brings results, but in few instances is promotion balanced by equal concern over the product that is promoted.

The positive value of all these faiths (and they are often practiced as religions) is not in question. But when carried to extremes, negative consequences result. Only when these polarized positions are replaced with open thinking, cooperation, collaboration, and innovation is a better tourism environment possible. Resource protection can and must be carried out concurrently with tourism development. Where properly designed and managed, the land can support both. Free enterprise, the very foundation of a market economy, is essential to tourism because it is responsive to market trends and provides jobs, income, tax revenues, and overall wealth. It can thrive in a setting that protects the resources on which tourism depends. Nonprofit groups perform valuable functions by increasing the protection and restoration of cultural resources while encouraging the development of services. Government agencies that have custody over resource areas fulfill their resource-protection objectives more fully when visitor use is properly designed and managed. In fact, their political support (such as for state and national parks) is strengthened when visitors are satisfied with the development available to them.

ROLE OF DESIGN

Where does the responsibility for tourism design lie? Certainly, landowners and developers need to become more sensitive to land and its role in tourism. Their choices of types, quantity, quality, and location govern most design decisions. Financial institutions also greatly influence design because they decide which projects are worthy of loans. But perhaps the greatest burden should be placed on professional designers. Those with the most influence are architects, landscape architects, engineers, sculptors, and interior designers. Also influential at times are philosophers, political scientists, economists, planners, horticulturalists, and painters.

While some professionals have recently developed a greater interest in tourism, the general level of understanding remains very low. Often a tourism job is approached by professionals with little design experience. Few schools of design include tourism land development in their curricula. So the need remains for environmental design enlightenment. As landscape architect Geoffrey Alan Jellicoe observed: "We know that nature left to herself becomes a jungle, and that is one of the purposes of our art to compose and order our environment to our particular requirements."[2]

The term *design* is used throughout this book rather than the term *planning* to emphasize the creative and artistic manipulation of structures and landscapes for the purpose of better tourism. This word choice suggests that everything that impinges on the traveler's senses—what he sees, hears, feels, smells, tastes, and moves through and over—is the responsibility of the designer. This attitude transcends all property boundaries and ownership jurisdictions. It commands us to view our travel world as a whole, knowing full well that thousands of independent decisions cause and influence that totality.

Approaching the travel landscape in this manner demands much from the entire design discipline and from all designers. Most manufactured products and even home environments are controlled by only one or a few designers. Not so for travel. Designers of transportation dictate how and what the traveler sees while in transit. The spatial relationship between seats, windows, and other factors governing comfort in planes, buses, and automobiles is critical to the travel experience. The design of drives, walks, lighting, and trails at parks, recreation areas, and forest reserves is

not only a matter of handling masses of people: these decisions dictate how the environment is experienced.

Of all the design professions, the one best suited to the task of environmental design for tourism is landscape architecture. That task can be carried out in several ways. First, landscape architects have training and experience in selecting and analyzing sites and generating design concepts for all land development. Second, the landscape architect can perform studies relating land characteristics to the requirements of owners and intended tourists. Third, landscape architects can communicate the results of these studies by means of public hearings, meetings, workshops, journals, and books. Finally, and perhaps most important, landscape architects can perform the critical role of catalyst, bringing together all parties that influence the design and development of tourism: owners, financiers, prospective managers, governmental regulators, other designers, and the many constituency groups affected by design. By not having a vested interest in the financing, ownership, or use of a completed project, the landscape architect can provide a broad, objective perspective. This role is traditional. As far back as 1858 Frederick Law Olmsted united the special concerns of several constituencies, the local political leadership, the consequences of urban growth, and New York City's natural resources to create Central Park.

## DESIGN CHALLENGE

Quietly, unobtrusively, but pervasively, tourism has risen to great socioeconomic heights in the United States and many other countries. Hundreds of thousands of workers depend on it for their livelihood. Thousands of governments rely on its tax revenues, which help support worthwhile services, such as education and welfare. Most of all, millions of travelers gain personal enrichment through travel. Travel is viewed as a human right and, except where prevented by terrorism or war, continues as a powerful social and economic force throughout the world.

# 2/

# Tourism Myopia

F ew places in the world have escaped the onslaught of tourists—defined in the broadest sense as people from one place who temporarily put themselves in another place and collectively spend millions of dollars doing it. Annually, over half of the people of the United States migrate from home to thousands of destinations here and abroad, where they carry on business or simply enjoy themselves among the amenities of different lands. What began as an incidental function of the home community (a desire and need to visit exotic places) has become a significant function of distant communities (a desire to obtain the economic gains that accrue from such temporary migrations).

The shift from accepting tourists as guests to catering to them as consumers has changed the face of the land. As developers of destination areas learned that tourists sought a variety of attractions, they began building- and land-development programs second to none.

## MASS TRAVEL CHAOS

Never before has there been the abundance and variety of environments now available to the tourist. As far as terrestrial travel is concerned, few frontiers remain, and soon this

also may be the case above and below the earth's surface.

With only slight alterations in a travel plan, a traveler can place himself in the heart of the remotest wilderness preserve or in the midst of one of the largest cities. His can be a romantic environment where sparkling streams run over rocky beds surrounded by quiet verdure. It can be a sports-centered environment where physical prowess is demonstrated on the ski slopes or in the surf. It can be a business-oriented destination.

## DEVELOPMENT COMPLEXITY

The opportunities for varied travel experiences today are self-evident. But critical in these times of boom expansion is the chaotic, confusing, awkward, and often downright ugly mass of development that characterizes so many travel environments. "Features of interest often lack all connectivity. Americans glory in the most arcane juxtapositions," says geographer David Lowenthal.[1] The sprawl of unrelated enterprise has responded to a need for unlimited access and has provided an abundance of varied land development, but the resulting tourist environment often misses its mark. After years of extensive travel in Egypt, landscape architect Hans Friedrich Werkmeister reported on the "carelessness and even the shamelessness by which so-called responsible people are pushing development of tourism to

Saint Augustine. (Photo courtesy St. Augustine & St. Johns County Chamber of Commerce)

7

Tourism environments too frequently are cluttered and despoil natural scenery, as shown here on the Appalachian Trail. (Photo courtesy National Park Service)

its most awkward lengths."[2] The blessing of unlimited access actually compounds the problem by compressing a large number of places into the traveler's experience. Ironically, this problem has missed the attention of politicians, planners, developers, and, especially, those who profit from tourism—business people.

The present unrelated and often bizarre mass of development has a very simple and logical explanation but little excuse. It is the result of independent decision making based on a myopic view of tourists by the many developers of land, public and private. Tourists are seen to be simply fried chicken eaters; boat, camera, lot, and RV buyers; and myriad other specific product consumers. The scattering of private and public land development reflects the fragmentation of this view. And it thus fails to represent an understanding of the tourist as a whole person, one whose actions and needs are consistent throughout his period of travel

and who seeks some continuity over the course of the experience. The multiplicity of development is not integrated to form a total personal environment from home to destination and back.

Over the past few decades some better travel environments have been provided to the public at their insistence. Before the days of freeways, jet planes, plastic money, and franchising, tourism was seen primarily as the business of catching the tourist on his way to a destination with a variety of appeals. It was a roadside phenomenon. The location and design of development almost entirely depended on visual impact—the more colorful and garish the better. Unsophisticated yet opportunistic entrepreneurs created an unrestrained roadside genre reflected in architecture, sites, and signs.

While much of this attitude remains, conditions are different today. More frequently, tourists make travel decisions at home, before

Business failure is often caused as much by poor location and design as by bad management.

leaving, rather than on impulse, along the way. Expressways, with their limited-access design, force travelers to stop for services at highway nodes. Jet travel and deregulation have stimulated greater air-terminal development. Credit cards, franchising, and toll-free telephoning have made travel-oriented facilities less dependent on impulse roadside purchases.

## CONSEQUENCES

The wealth and sprawl of modern travel development of the environment is at once a blessing and a problem. The lack of a comprehensive design for new developments places many restraints on opportunity. "Bad enough that the left hand has not known what the right hand has been doing: the one hand has frequently chopped the other off at the wrist," states a Canadian tourism official.[3] Tourists are limited in their efforts to gain the greatest satisfaction in exchange for the time, money, and energy they have invested. Resources are more heavily eroded, and public and private investors miss opportunities for greater success.

The private business ideology, which upholds the right of entrepreneurs to succeed or fail on their own terms, sometimes places businesses in peculiar locations and sites with disastrous consequences. Plentiful are the financial failures of northern cottage resorts that were built on property the owner merely liked, hunted on, or had inherited rights to. Farmers, intending to bolster sagging farm enterprise, have often been disappointed with their ventures into recreational businesses on their lands. Their agricultural expertise was insufficient for success in a recreational enterprise. Many tourism business people have relied more heavily on their own intuition than on facts. Frequently, land prices or easy terms of purchase have put businesses in the wrong places. Owner bias rather than sensitivity to markets has produced design as well as business failures. Most often, business people have mistakenly opposed the establishment of major parks devoted to scenery, wildlife, or historical themes—the very magnets that might have drawn markets for their commercial services. Owners, public and private, are missing great tourism opportunities because of their narrow and fragmented vision.

Furthermore, the narrow look often leads to the destruction of the very resource base upon which tourism is founded. Water pollution is a long-standing problem, but contrary to the views of many who seek to solve it, big industry is not the only threat to this important resource. Developers of tourist services, such as lodging and dining, are too often the ones who whittle away at such resources as beautiful views, open park spaces, and clean beaches. For example, lakeshore subdividers who have greater concern for sales than for protection of beach quality pour raw sewage into swimming waters, aggravate boat congestion, and spoil the aesthetic values highly regarded by their potential customers. The wonders that lure people to spend their money at these business places are continuously weakened until, finally, the public fails to return.

Unique land characteristics of slope, surface soils, trees, and other plant materials are bulldozed away, and sterile and monotonous sites

are produced, if unintentionally. Landscape architect Adolf Schmitt observed after visiting the Nile:

> As the objects worth seeing are slowly given away to destruction, the one-sided development of tourism leads itself to absurdum. First of all the exaggerated traffic handling: the "Valley of Kings" is covered with asphalt and concrete right into the center, which today is occupied by a monstrous restaurant building, suitably called the "Tomb of Coca Cola." There the tumultuous, eating and noisily drinking human mass is sitting right in the middle of one of the most time-honored and most ancient graveyards of this world.[4]

This visual as well as physical erosion of the travel landscape is contributed to by an excessive use of billboards. "Twirling, flapping, flashing signs line our streets and jar our senses. . . . The purveyors of visual pollution have been given rein to spread chaos and blight along our streets and across our land."[5]

Finally, and perhaps most important, the myopic approach to land development reduces the opportunity for visitors to obtain the pleasurable objectives they seek (fig. 2-1). They seek roadside scenery, not roadside clutter; too often ugliness and disorder are all they find. They seek clear and safe waters in which to swim, fish, and boat—not water that is dirty and refuse-laden. They seek long vistas and romantic landscapes, scenes to photograph

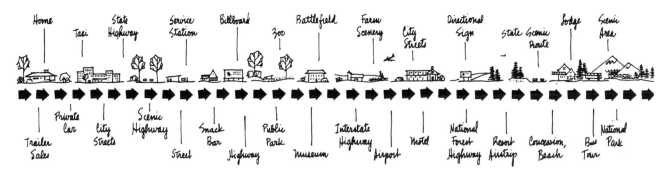

**2-1.** *Tourism environments.* It is essential for designers and developers to understand the traveler's flow through the landscape.

and views to remember. They do not seek "concrete jungles" of high-rise structures that insulate them from waterfront breezes and views.

Park decision makers often ignore the user's needs for commercial services. Commercial interests often ignore the user's desire for the recreational opportunities traditionally provided by public agencies, such as parks, beaches, and campgrounds. What is created and managed in the environment has much to do with the user's peace of mind.

All designers and developers of tourism should have a sharper and broader consciousness of the visitor's total environment. Emphasis on individual projects is natural and even essential if they are to succeed. However, recognition of the personal desires, habits, and tastes of travelers, and accommodation of these traveler characteristics, is even more critical. If participants are not satisfied, development has failed.

Recognition of the present status of total development is the first step toward improvement. Again, based on his visits to Egypt, Werkmeister observed:

> One could count up all these large and small bits of dreadfulness, but the question remains: who is responsible? Perhaps all of them—the ministries, the administrators of antiquities, the archeologists, egyptologists, architects, restorers . . . all of them. But I think most of them do not feel it. They share a total insensitivity to the ensemble, to the real damage they have done to the great antiquities . . . Obviously, no landscape architect was consulted.[6]

Fortunately, developers and owners occupy much more common ground than they would lead us to believe. If they join forces to investigate how people and land relate to form a broad, functioning system, the first effort essential to the improvement of overall tourism design will have been accomplished.

## THE FUNCTIONAL TOURISM SYSTEM

Worldwide, the concept of tourism has come to mean everything associated with travel, from the experiences desired by travelers through the policies, programs, and physical development required to stimulate and accommodate such travel. This sweeping concept, seductively simple to nations and regions seeking to bolster sagging economies, is in fact extremely complicated.

When a state, province, or country contemplates improvement and expansion of tourism development, it has to consider tourism in its totality, not just a few parts. Even though successful operation of each part is essential, equally important is how the many parts interrelate. The problems of integration are exacerbated by the marked differences between tourism and other economic development.

For one thing, tourism distributes markets to products (travel destinations) rather than the opposite pattern of goods that are distributed to markets from points of manufacture. This difference means that the product areas, the places to which we travel, are more difficult to plan, design, and manage.

For the traveler, these places mean everything, whereas the place of manufacture of hard goods is of no concern to the consumer. The tourism product is not canned or shrink-wrapped but, rather, a collection of experiences gained by the traveler. Therefore, it is more complicated and far more challenging to design than a can of peas.

Tourism, therefore, is indigenous; it is of and by the land. For tourism, the natural and built environment varies throughout the nation. Some areas have more settings of interest to travelers than do others. The location of a manufacturing plant is less dependent on such settings.

Because tourism development at the regional, state, or national scale includes thousands of properties and their owners, it is difficult to realize how they may be interrelated. If the problems of poor connectivity and integration are to be solved, a broad perspective of how tourism functions is critical. Tourist organizations and agencies at the larger scale could be more instrumental in increasing coordination and integration of tourism if tourism is planned in its functional entirety rather than merely through its separate parts.

One way of gaining insight into how tourism functions is through a scenario of a trip from home to destination and back. The tourist's experience begins when he determines the season and length of his vacation, often dictated by an employer. The travel itinerary depends on many informational and promotional factors. For example, the anecdotes of a friend, a magazine article, an advertisement of a vacation package, or a book or movie may influence the selection of a destination. Personal preference may influence the choice between a touring-circuit or resort-type vacation. Income and personal preference may influence the mode of travel—tent camping, RV, historical tours, air, cruise, or personal car. If an air travel or motorcoach package is selected, a travel agent will probably book the entire vacation or such portions as air travel.

On the way, the auto traveler makes many decisions on places for food, lodging, and car service. The need may arise for banking, telephone, or health service facilities en route. Throughout the trip the traveler will rely on maps, signs, and guidance from local residents for directions. Based on planning before leaving home or impulse along the way, stops at attractions may be added to the touring circuit. The RV traveler is likely to visit natural-resource sites en route to a destination, enjoying the flora and fauna of parks and recreation areas.

The experiences obtained depend on the successful match between the availability of attractions and the traveler's preference. For example, if a community has restored many of its historic buildings, developed an outdoor drama of its history, and replicated period crafts for sale, history buffs may make sure they visit there. Public agencies that manage extensive forests, lakes, and wildlife resources may attract many visitors to view, photograph, or become enriched by natural-resource environments, even though resource protection is their main objective.

Other traveler segments may choose urban destinations because of their special attractions. Historic sites, entertainment, specialty food places, museums, theme parks, sports arenas, and the homes of friends and relatives attract visitors seeking the particular experiences afforded by these places. Of course, convention centers, trade centers, and a variety of business and professional offices make cities the objectives of business travelers.

Upon returning home, the traveler reflects on the experience. Discussion with friends and relatives reveals the extent to which the trip fulfilled expectations. The greatest adventure may have come from difficulties encountered along the way. Through snapshots, color slides, and souvenirs the trip is relived and related to others. The success or failure of the experience may have a great influence on next year's trip plans.

As can be seen by this description, there may be a great many travel scenarios, because segments of the population have different preferences for travel experiences. Compared to expenditures of time and money on other activities and goods, travel must have high priority. Furthermore, one must have an income sufficient for travel.

The point of this discussion is to demonstrate that overall travel involves many business establishments, many public places, and many programs by organizations and agencies directed toward specific functions. This complexity of different places and programs functions well only when each individual part is designed and managed so that it *relates well to others*, in addition to carrying out its individual, primary function. It is not enough, for example, that a hotel has good facilities and services and is well managed. Unless it is accessible and related to the surrounding attractions that bring visitors, it is not carrying out its complete function. It is a lack of interrelation between the many parts that has often caused travel difficulties. While the designer cannot solve all such problems, much improvement could be accomplished through design relevance to many external factors. The interrelationships among the many parts suggests that there is some overall functioning of tourism that binds it together in a system.

It is important for designers to recognize market segmentation. Some segments prefer sports activities, such as swimming or surfing at the Assateague Island National Seashore. (Photo courtesy National Park Service)

Other segments of the market have different interests, such as cultural appreciation. (Photo of Gettysburg National Military Park: Richard Frear, courtesy National Park Service)

The National Park Service offers attractions for visitors and also protects environmental assets. (Photo of Yellowstone National Park: William S. Keller, courtesy National Park Service)

Figure 2-2 is a model of the functional tourism system. This model sweeps all functioning tourism elements into five interrelated components. Conceptually it borrows from economics by showing a *market* side interrelated with a *supply* side. While designers, planners, and land developers are concerned primarily with the supply side, they are subject to the many characteristics of the market side. This market-supply model is not merely a tourism industry model. It encompasses the develop-

ment and programs of all three sectors— business, nonprofit organizations and governments (as developers). The market side encompasses the component of *population*, and the supply side encompasses four components: *transportation, attractions, services,* and *information/promotion.*

Within the *population* component are all people with an interest in and ability to travel. The *transportation* component includes all modes—air, personal car, motorcoach, tour, cruise ship, RV, taxi, and rental car. Labeled *attractions* are all the places that provide both the pulling power to travel away from home and the satisfaction achieved therefrom. The *services* component includes businesses related to travel, such as lodging, food service, car service, and shops. Within the *information/promotion* component are activities, programs, and physical development that offer several forms of promotion and provide information and directions for the traveler.

Chapter 3 provides elaboration of the important characteristics of travel markets. Attraction functions and design implications are described in Chapter 4. Important design aspects of transportation, services, and information/promotion are described in many other parts of the book. However, the following comments highlight some of the design aspects of these last three components.

Transportation

Although the application of technology to transportation modes in the last few decades has greatly improved many aspects of travel, many consumer difficulties remain. The manyfold increase in speed of jet planes over earlier propeller-driven planes has stimulated the use of destinations never before accessible. Shorter periods of time in the air and less upset by turbulence have increased traveler comfort. Automobile design and construction have produced more efficient and comfortable cars. The divided freeway concept has allowed much greater volume of traffic and at the same time has reduced the rate of accidents. Tourism would not have become such a dominant worldwide phenomenon had it not been for these improvements. Even so, changes are needed. It does seem that there is much travail in today's travel, just as described by Jerome Turler in the sixteenth century: "Nothing else but a painstaking to see and search for foreine landes, not to be taken in hande by all sorts of persons or inadvisedly, but as are meete thereto."[7]

The miracle of jet travel is often offset by difficulties with which only the calloused veteran can cope: missed connections, overbook-

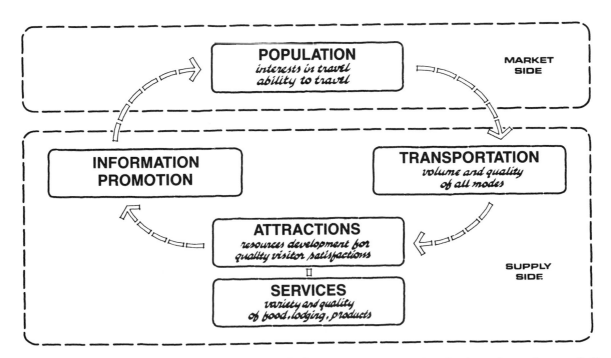

**2-2.** *The functional tourism system.* Designers and planners must recognize the interdependence of all components (and their constituent parts) and integrate them to create an overall functioning system.

While the technology and engineering of travel have improved greatly since the 1920s, travel can still be complicated and frustrating. (Photo courtesy Texas State Department of Highways and Public Transportation)

ing, pilot errors, mechanical problems, controller errors, chaotic terminals, and even hijacking. The miracle of freeway travel is offset by poor directional signage, drunk and otherwise impaired drivers, truck-driver bullying, and the violence of some frustrated drivers. Within cities, the application of traffic engineering has improved traffic flow at the expense of livability and, especially, pedestrian use of downtown. Many years ago it was learned that the economic benefits of tourism are not derived from people in motion—visitors must have the opportunity to stop, leave their vehicles, and enjoy the amenities on foot.

Those who own, design, and operate transportation systems used by tourists have a narrow view of users because of the limitations of their agencies. Highway planners, for example, improve highways only when accident rates increase, rather than when new developments create new demands. Highway officials usually see travelers as part of a mechanical flow diagram, with each mile of concrete ribbon calculated on the basis of so many rubber-tired steel units per hour. Airline officials generally regard travelers as point-to-point cargo, to be made airborne at one place and then grounded at another at the fastest possible speed. Airport decision makers are mainly concerned with servicing aircraft; passenger ticketing, toileting, and feeding; and lost-baggage-processing. And all of this is done within

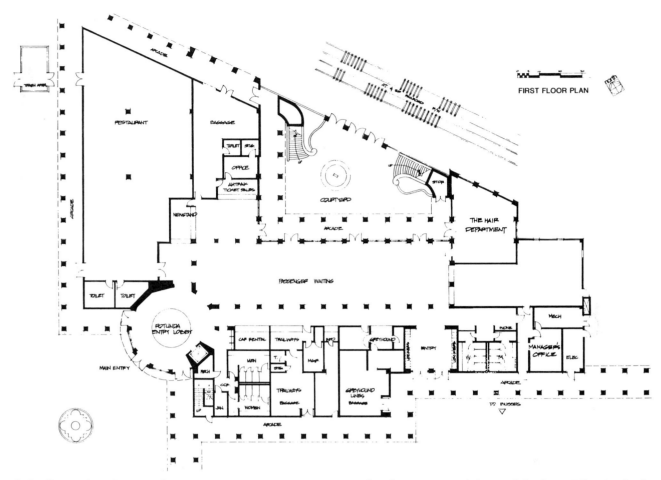

**2-3.** *Santa Ana Regional Transportation Center.* An example of an intermodal travel facility. (The Burlock Partnership, architects.)

heavily invested capital improvement programs that are only incidentally related to attractions, other transportation modes, or the regional tourism environment.

Intermodal travel facilities, a feature of European cities for many years, are increasingly being constructed in the United States.[8] These transportation centers ease the traveler's shift from one transportation mode to another. For example, over half a million travelers a year pass through the Santa Ana Regional Transportation Center in California, which connects Amtrak trains to the Orange County Transit District and Greyhound bus services, the Camino Real Express (which runs between Orange County and the Tijuana, Mexico, air-

port), limousines and airport shuttles, taxi services, and personal cars (fig. 2-3). The center is conveniently located. It has balconies and observation decks, a restaurant, a bar, a barbershop, and over four hundred parking spaces. And it is attractively and appropriately designed with respect both to building and site. Other cities have developed intermodal facilities—Sacramento, California; Charleston, South Carolina; Pontiac, Michigan; Kalamazoo, Michigan; and Harrisburg, Pennsylvania. These centers not only aid travelers but often stimulate the reuse of historic depots and the development of new shopping centers and the business complexes surrounding them.

## Services/Facilities

Individual building and landscape designs for tourist services have gradually improved, in part because of increased public demand for better quality. Franchises and corporate developments, as compared with "mom-pop" establishments, can now afford sophisticated market surveys. For fast food places, this has resulted in subdued colors of interiors and exteriors, better building styles, and better landscape development. Some motel and restaurant chains, yielding to local demands for the adaptation of commercial establishments to particular environments, have more than one design for sites, buildings, and signs.

Even so, individual decision making generally remains nearsighted rather than broad-visioned, and the free enterprise system is not responsible for this myopic view. Rather, a lack of understanding of the true nature of each business purpose and a misconception of the product are at fault.

There is a difference between a travel "product" and a manufactured product. Whereas for tourism the market is distributed among hundreds of destinations, each of which is a small portion of the total product, for manufactured goods the product is contained in one package and distributed to markets. Most consumers of the latter type of merchandise have no notion of where the vegetables they eat are grown or the clothing they wear is made. Conversely, the location of the tourism product is an absolute that is at the very heart of tourism. Improvement in the quality of land development for tourism will not come through regulation and control as much as through the individual property developer's understanding of tourists—the very people for whom the property is being developed.

The design and development of lodging remains narrowly site-oriented. To satisfy the several market segments, the new generation of lodging ranges from bed-and-breakfast and budget motels to luxury hotels with large suites and hot tubs. However, owners and managers of lodging continue to be preoccupied with operations within the site at the expense of understanding many external influences on their success. Room sales are as dependent on access, relation to attractions, and neighborhood amenities as on the quality of the hotel. Unfortunately, neither educational institutions nor trade associations emphasize these external factors.

Commercial services for travelers greatly overlap those for residents. Restaurants, car service stations, and shops are used both by resident and travel markets. Even hotels, catering primarily to travelers, frequently have resident services, such as restaurants, gift shops, and banquet rooms. However, urban planners and designers tend to consider only resident functions of commercial services in plans.

Here and there across the land, as illustrated further in this book, designers and owners of services for travelers are becoming more sensitive to the need for better, more relevant design. Exterior and interior designs of hotels, restaurants, and shops are beginning to reflect regional themes—verdant, desert, ethnic, historic. For example, old decorative iron facades along the Strand in Galveston (once a warehouse district) not only retain the 1890s theme but also lead the visitor to modern food services and tourist gift shops inside.

The services component of the tourism system deserves greater design attention for a better relationship between tourist sites and surrounding visitor functions and landscapes.

## Information/Promotion

State and national tourism agencies usually carry on programs of information and promotion as if they were the same; for this reason they are lumped together as one component. However, more careful scrutiny of these functions shows their difference. Even though information and promotion are generally outside the realm of design, some implications are worthy of consideration.

There are several reasons for increased concern over the topic of travel information today. The explosion in the number of places to visit, due to easier access and the greater propensity

Shopping continues as a very important aspect of tourism. (Photo of Fiesta Gardens, Austin, Texas, courtesy Texas State Department of Highways and Public Transportation)

of people to travel, has increased confusion on the part of the potential traveler. There are so many more choices and so many more promotional pieces and advertisements that travel decisions are harder to make. The growth of travel agent services, guide books, and guided motorcoach tours bears testimony to the acceptance of new and better travel information.

Because most travel market segments are more sophisticated today—both in terms of education and travel experience—they are seeking more and better information. They are no longer satisfied with merely being exposed to an attraction. If it is a historic site, they want more description of the site's relevance to events of the period. If travelers are visiting outdoor recreation areas, they want more in-

formation on how to hunt, fish, or photograph wildlife. Because the population has become more urbanized, there is no longer the close contact with nature common to previous generations, and more things need explanation.

Land and building designers now have an important role in fostering better information for visitors. Current travel destination planning and design incorporate greater installation of interpretation functions. In the fields of outdoor recreation and tourism, the term *interpretation* has come to encompass "a service for visitors to parks, forests, refuges and similar recreation areas."[9] Astute landscape and building architects are creating new visitor centers and ancillary services, such as trailside information, to handle mass tourism at park sites.

Included often within the centers are exhibits, dioramas, demonstrations, and lectures. Often trails are designed to bring the visitor into close proximity to special features of the landscape. Along the way, numbered stops, keyed to explanations in an information booklet, help the visitor understand the environment. When properly designed, such interpretive areas can provide a great number of visitors with satisfying experiences without disturbing and eroding resources. In other words, a high percentage of travel markets are satisfied with a somewhat vicarious experience that does not demand close contact with or disturbance of natural and cultural resources.

A continuing controversial issue is the use of roadside signs. A spokesman for the Coalition for Scenic Beauty states, "America the beautiful is becoming America the ugly, the home of billboards, flashing signs, and endless clutter."[10] Because the experience of viewing roadside scenery continues to rate high in travel surveys it seems incumbent upon designers of highway corridors to keep them attractive. Generally, travelers prefer natural resource vistas, farm landscapes, and well-maintained structures over excessive billboards, junk yards, and dilapidated buildings.

On the other hand travelers do seek information as they travel. They need enough highway signs to direct their course, and they need some means of identifying locations of services and attractions. A more collaborative study by designers, planners, highway engineers, and local government agencies responsible for roadside zoning is necessary to fulfill these needs.

## INTERLACINGS

This introduction to the tourism functional system is meant to underscore design interrelationships among the many parts of the entire tourism phenomenon. All parts are related to other parts, as evidenced by the flow of travelers. Integration with other parts must be an objective of the design process of any one part.

For example, it is insufficient for a designer of a restaurant to be guided only by narrow food-service functions. The design must be sensitive to trends in market changes and the influence of surrounding landscape development, access, and other tourism functions. The design must reflect the needs and desires both of local and travel markets.

It is clear that in order to achieve such desired integration of design, developers will require much greater communication and cooperation among themselves. This is not easily accomplished, because of the need for specialized investment and development on a multiplicity of properties. It is doubtful whether governmental intervention or legal regulation can force design integration. Rather, as the individual owners and developers increasingly recognize their dependence on decisions made by others in the tourism system, they will understand that their self-interest will be served through greater communication and understanding. Designers can then respond by fulfilling a catalytic role, bringing the interests of developers, tourists, and environmentalists into harmony.

As a tourism function, promotion differs from information because its purpose is to alert and persuade, not necessarily to inform. Within the field of promotion, practitioners now generally include four forms: advertising (paid space in such media as print, television, and radio), nonpaid publicity (such as magazine articles), public relations (personal contact), and incentives (discounts, give-aways). Most of these functions are beyond the responsibility of land and architectural design. However, designers could improve the effectiveness and reliability of promotion if they intervened in the process of developing it. Too often promotion, developed in offices quite removed from destinations and attractions, offers overblown images to travelers. The actual experience cannot measure up to promises in the slick puffery of the promoters. Design professions can perform a catalytic role by making sure that the promotion and the real travel objectives are in accord.

## CONCLUSIONS

The great growth of tourism, providing many more millions of people with travel experiences, has had its toll. As developers have rushed to provide the attractions, transportation, and services for tourists undertaking both business and pleasure travel, functional and environmental issues have arisen.

The resulting built environment is often chaotic, confusing, and ugly—not by willful intent but most often by accident of juxtaposition of separate site design and development. The very expansion required to serve more tourists has stumbled on itself in the process. As a consequence business is less successful than it might be, visitors do not gain full satisfaction from their travels, and the environment suffers, physically and aesthetically.

Designers can do much to remedy this situation. First, they can insist on better educational programs in the design field. Where curricula include subjects emphasizing the interrelationship between individual businesses and their surroundings, designers will be better qualified to carry out integrated design in their work. Second, in their regular professional practice, they can provide the setting for early interaction between developers of sites and others of important relevance. Office conferences that enable the several interests to exchange ideas and plans can provide functional design guidance. Finally, designers can do more to publicize exemplary designs that reflect better integration among the several functional components. There is nothing as convincing as an accomplished fact.

# 3/

# Travelers, Public Involvement, and Design

**B**ehavioral science, particularly as it relates to tourists, seems peripheral to the art of the landscape designer and architect. We look to designers for innovation and that rare gift of artistic talent. We expect them to give us poetry in the structures, landscapes, and sculpture of our built physical world. Inherent in the design process is a realization of the designer's goals. Yet it is hollow for the designer to satisfy his own ego without benefitting society as a whole. The public that uses the environment should be the final judge.

For centuries designers have overwhelmingly directed their attention to localite, not traveler, functions. In today's world this is insufficient. The designer requires more current information about tourists. In some ways they may be similar to local residents, but in others they are quite different.

In addition to travelers, several other public groups influence design. Within any state, province, city, or village, owners or designers do not have sole power of decision over what is developed. Often the attitudes and perceptions of the different ethnic, economic, religious, environmental, and racial groups in communities have fostered or halted tourist development. Public officials, influenced by regulations or opinion, also have had direct bearing on decisions regarding the design and development of tourism.

The importance to design of the images, activities, and characteristics of tourists, as well as the attitudes and actions of other public groups, are discussed in this chapter.

## TOURISTS AND IMAGES

All of us have images of destinations, whether or not we have traveled to them. These images may be sharp or vague, factual or whimsical, but in all cases they are indicative of likes and dislikes. By means of many communication inputs throughout our lifetime—advertising, radio, television, magazines, books, comments from friends and relatives—we accumulate such images and assign values to them, good or bad. And although they arise from general information about the designed environment, these images are always highly personal.

### Resources Are Not—They Become

Nature has not always been considered beautiful. Hans Huth relates a description Father Hennepin wrote of Niagara Falls in 1679: "The Waters which fall from this vast height, do foam and boyl after the most hideous manner

Big Bend National Park. (Photo courtesy Texas State Department of Highways and Public Transportation)

23

imaginable, making an outrageous noise, more terrible than that of thunder. . . . Dismal roaring may be heard above fifteen leagues off."[1] The "hideous" sight has become a major tourist attraction for millions and is now considered one of the most beautiful spots in North America. The very same lakes, mountains, and forests now used heavily by tourists and vacationers did not have a recreational value for the Puritans, who adopted "the strictest regulations 'in detestation of idleness' to the end of enforcing work and prohibiting all amusements."[2]

Physical land characteristics become resources only when they are so attributed by society. "Neither the environment as such nor parts or features of the environment *per se* are resources; they become resources only if, when, and in so far as they are, or considered to be capable of serving man's needs. In other words, the word 'resource' is an expression of appraisal and, hence, a purely subjective concept."[3] Through travelers' perceptions we can learn more about how land qualities become tourism resources.

## Image Origins

Deeper exploration of the image phenomenon reveals that a region's images are of two levels. The first might be called the *organic* image level. A report of Alaska's tourism is typical of this level of image development. "Most of our vacationers have been quietly assimilating impressions and information about Alaska for a number of years, and we cannot say what triggered them [the vacationers] to come."[4]

Many images are the result of readers' assimilation of material from newspapers, periodicals, and books. Children's geography and history books are probably the most influential in the early formation of images. Such places as Jamestown, Plymouth, and New York, whose colonial histories are colorfully described in elementary texts, bear resonances that undoubtedly carry over into adulthood. The mere mention of these places in later years evokes images that become important to travel.

The second level of tourist images derives from a conscious effort to develop, promote, and advertise. These are *induced* images. Advertising literature, magazine articles, guidebooks, television promotion, travel tour packages, and promotion by travel businesses overtly provide us with images of places.

A distinction is drawn between these two levels of images to separate images that can be influenced by designers and developers from those that cannot. It is possible that the designed environment has more to do with our perception of places than all the efforts of marketers and advertisers.

## Image Psychology Applied

The development of a relationship between things and their images in the minds of people has been explained by psychologist Jerome S. Bruner as a three-phase process: *hypothesis*, *input*, and *check*.[5] A review of how this process applies to tourism may assist in relating environmental design of the vacationscape to users.

*Hypothesis.* People appear to bring as much to a tourism experience as they receive from a given stimulus in the environment, such as a mountain, campfire, or waterfall. This complicated psychological phenomenon is explained rather simply by architect Eugene Raskin: "Our heads are crowded with ideas and associations in a way that may be likened to a random card index file, voluminous and untidy, but cross referenced way down to the subconscious."[6]

Hypothesis, or expectancy, explains many of the varied reactions different people have from the same stimulus. For example, one person, familiar with the ways of birds, may spot an eagle's nest more than three hundred yards away, whereas another, unfamiliar with ornithology, may see it as merely a misshapen branch.

Expectancy gains strength in several ways: confirmation, monopoly, and consequences.[7] The more that a travel experience has been confirmed, the more confident the user is of potential satisfaction when he considers re-

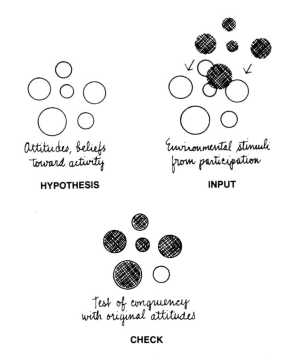

**HYPOTHESIS** — *Attitudes, beliefs toward activity*

**INPUT** — *Environmental stimuli from participation*

**CHECK** — *Test of congruency with original attitudes*

**3-1.** *Travel image psychology.* Three steps in the traveler's experience test the "fit" between visitor images and development.

peating the experience. In fact, an image is generally very resistant to change if it is pleasant or meets expectations. Sometimes this impression is strengthened by a lifetime of repeated confirmation. Scholars have shown that the maturation of images requires both the physical and mental maturity of the individual. In other words, developing habits is part of maturity. If this were not true, daily life would completely consume our energies because every act—even rising in the morning—would require a multitude of new and separate decisions.

Once made, habits are hard to break. Innovations in tourism can be difficult to sustain. "The larger the negative value that we give to uncertainty or to vagueness in our value orientation, the more likely we are to select the familiar and the known."[8] Tourists are likely to see what they anticipate seeing, and the designer must be aware of these expectations in designing the environment.

"The closer to monopoly a hypothesis is, the less information will be required to confirm it and the more tenaciously will it be retained in the face of stimulus contradiction."[9] An example of the monopolistic in this application is Disneyland. Nearly all early attempts to duplicate this attraction met with little success. Even though they provided many similar amusements and entertainments, one element was missing—the monopoly of the name Disney. For most Americans that name has come to mean a high level of performance and a high probability of success.

Furthermore, the hypothesis is strengthened by the anticipation of consequences.[10] For example, if a fisherman has found that a stream with a certain combination of attributes —location, size, flow, and setting—has usually been productive for trout fishing, the expectancy of similar catches is strong when similar stream conditions are met. Moreover, if personal motivation is strong—if the fisherman is avid to make a big catch—expectancy is further enforced. "Stimulation does not fall on a passive receiver. The individual, on the contrary, is 'prepared,' implicitly or explicitly, for certain kinds of input; the input is actively dealt with on the basis of this preparation. The fate of any input is at least partly dependent on the nature of the preparation."[11]

*Input.* In the passage just quoted, Bruner refers to the second phase of image formation, the individual's immediate reaction to a stimulus, or the *input process.* Direct exposure to such stimuli as a scenic view or historic restoration produces a sensory reaction. We gain input through the several senses, and the response is highly complex. Indeed, instead of the traditional five senses, Samuel Howard Bartley describes ten sense modalities: vision, hearing, pressure and touch, temperature, kinesthesis, pain, taste, smell, vestibular sense, and common chemical sense.[12] Moreover, experiments document the interrelation of several senses in response to a single stimulus. Whereas a single sense, such as vision, may dominate one's perception of a vacationscape, others are also intertwined. For example, one experiences a mountain climb through the lungs and leg muscles as much as through the eyes. Likewise, an ocean conveys as much meaning from the sound of the waves, the smell of the water, and the touch of the breeze, as from the visual appeal of a colorful and scintillating sunset reflected in the water. Even in complete darkness a person "sees" by means of touching objects.

The totality of sensuous experience leaves enduring impressions. For example, the sight of a fort reconstruction, with attendants dressed in period costume, combined with the sounds and smell of gunpowder exploding in a cannon that had been used at the fort in former times, all provide a complex range of sensations.

When one creates the stimuli related to regional tourism, concern cannot be limited to a single sense modality. Only by anticipating the quality of the input can a designer mold the environment to fully satisfy visitors.

*Check.* Finally, seeing is not necessarily believing. Input—sensations received from a stimulus—is checked against the expected image, which is then either confirmed or infirmed. Evidence suggests that the strength or weakness of the original hypothesis has much to do with the success of input from the stimulus.

When psychological check does not equal hypothesis, there is letdown. Such was the case for Steinbeck when he crossed the Continental Divide.

Interpreted in vacationscape terms this theory means, for example, that two people could experience the same boat tour quite differently. One person may have had a very strong expectancy, possibly based on having seen color slides and having heard the narration of a close friend who described the event in glowing terms. Another person may have had no more than a brief description by a service station attendant a few minutes before taking the trip. The imagery of the first person may have been overstimulated, resulting in disappointment after it was compared with the actual experience. The second person may have been well pleased because the quality of the input was superior to expectation. Several variables appear to be working at the same time—differences in kind and strength of hypotheses and differences in the backgrounds of the participants.

Author John Steinbeck relates a travel experience illustrating the element of check:

> I remember as a child reading or hearing the words "The Great Divide" and being stunned by the glorious sound, a proper sound for the granite backbone of the continent. I saw in my mind escarpments rising into the clouds, a kind of natural Great Wall of China. . . . Were it not for a painted sign I never would have known when I crossed it. . . . The place wasn't impressive enough to carry a stupendous fact like that.[13]

A rich description of how input is checked against a previous image is the account of Henry James following his visit to Mount Vernon, a tourist attraction in the context of this study:

> The old high-placed house, unquestionably, is charming, and the felicity of the whole scene, on such a day as that of my impression, scarce to be uttered. . . . Association does, at Mount Vernon, simply what it likes with us—it is of so beautiful and noble a sort; and to this end it begins by making us unfit to say whether or not we would in its absence have noticed the house for any material grace at all. . . . The whole thing *is* Washington—not his invention . . . and his property, but his presence and his person; with discriminations (as distinguished from enthusiasms) as invidious and unthinkable as if they were addressed to his very ears. . . . Thus we arrive at the full meaning, as it were —thus know, at least, why we are so moved.[14]

On the other hand, Henry James's visit to Washington's home, Mount Vernon, exceeded his expectations. (Photo courtesy Virginia Department of Conservation and Economic Development)

## OTHER CONSUMER BEHAVIOR THEORIES

Another basic theory of consumer behavior was advanced several years ago by John A. Howard and Jagdish N. Sheth.[15] This theory contains four major components acting in sequence: stimulus variables, response variables, hypothetical constructs, and exogenous variables. The stimulus variables, such items as price, quality, service, distinctiveness, and availability, are as important to travel as to other purchases. Among the response variables described are attention, comprehension, attitude, intention to buy, and actual purchase behavior. The hypothetical constructs fall into two classes: those having to do with perception, and those having to do with learning. Perceptual constructs serve the function of information-processing; learning constructs serve the function of concept-formation. The exogenous variables are personal, social, and cultural. Past influences are embedded here as in hypothetical constructs. All components are in dynamic interaction throughout the process.

Other behavioral theorists, such as Harold H. Kassarjian, do not adhere to stimulus-response concepts, emphasizing instead such factors as memory, expectations, and goal-seeking. They believe that "the individual acquires habits not only by repetition of stimulus and response but also by using insight, thinking, and problem-solving techniques."[16] Others subscribe neither to stimulus-response nor cognitive theories, but place greater emphasis on need systems, personality, and learning systems.

The applicability of consumer behavior research to the purchase of hard goods is not yet fully confirmed for services. The tourism product side is a complicated mix of goods and services. A. Parasuraman has identified three major differences that set services apart from goods: intangibility, heterogeneity, and inseparability.[17] Services are performances, not objects. They vary from performer to performer, so consistency is difficult to ensure. The production and consumption functions are inseparable: the consumer's input is as critical as that of the service's provider.

Based on executive and focus-group interviews (of nontouristic enterprises), Parasuraman identified ten dimensions of service quality:

reliability
responsiveness
competence
access
courtesy

communication
credibility
security
understanding/knowing
  the customer
tangibles (for example,
  physical facilities)

While the majority of these dimensions are outside the design realm, tangibles—the appearance and functioning of the designed environment—are important aspects related to tourist behavior.

## TOURIST CHARACTERISTICS

If the images, values, and behavior of tourists are so important, how can they be documented to assist designers and developers of physical places? Over the years, marketers and behaviorists have believed that there is sufficient correlation between the characteristics, preferences, and activities of travelers to apply certain measures. For example, research is revealing that some correlation exists between tourist activites and psychographics and lifestyles. But the complexity of human behavior, especially travelers' behavior, has made this task difficult. Following is a brief description of some of the factors that may assist designers in creating places that fulfill the needs of visitors.

### Design Relevance Unclear

Studies of tourists usually present information about *who* they are, *what* they do, and *why* they do it. One may well presume that developers and managers, armed with results from these studies, are in a better position to develop and market tourism. Unfortunately, the designer will not find pertinent information

neatly organized or presented in ways most applicable to design decisions. Access to this information is further complicated by the nature of organizations doing the studies. Generally, market research data obtained by national tourism offices are not made available to the general public.

As a nonprofit organization, the U.S. Travel Data Center makes most of its findings on national travel available to the public, but it also conducts several proprietary studies. Some states and provinces of the United States and Canada conduct studies of tourists, but they do not always publish results for designers and developers. Businesses undertake their own proprietary research and almost never make it public. Increasingly, academic departments in universities conduct research on travelers, which is reported in the United States in two tourism journals: *The Annals of Tourism Research* and *The Journal of Travel Research*. In addition, annual volumes of proceedings from conferences of the Travel and Tourism Research Association contain information on tourist characteristics. *Tourism Management*, a journal published in England, and occasional reports of the World Tourism Organization, issued from Madrid, also report on travel studies.

Frequently, tourist studies seek to find information about origins-destinations, employment generated, attractions visited, and reasons for travel. It is the future responsibility of the design professions to seek out current information from other specialists on the dynamics of the tourist—the demand side. Following is a very cursory review of the types of information designers and developers can now obtain about tourists.

### Demographics

In the 1970s studies of tourists focused primarily on demographics—age, sex, income, education and occupation. These descriptors were thought to be useful in marketing tourism. More recent studies, however, have shown little correlation between demographic variables and tourist activities, with some notable exceptions. For example, the very poor cannot travel, whereas affluent persons travel farther and more frequently and spend more money on travel in proportion to their wealth. In recent years the significant increase in life span combined with earlier retirement has produced more potential travelers in the upper age brackets.

Older populations are not all alike in their travel interests. Generally, however, they dominate overseas travel and use recreation vehicles, package tours, and air travel more frequently than younger travelers do. However, they often prefer the same kinds of experiences as younger travelers.[18]

Economics

Studies stimulated by state and provincial tourist agencies seeking legislative funding focus primarily on economic impact. Many econometric models have been put forward to measure the complicated expenditures on travel. Indeed, as individual states undertook such research in this country, it soon became impossible to make comparisons or obtain national data because of the diversity of formulas. In 1973 the U.S. Travel Data Center was formed and an economic model designed. For the first time a model produced reliable and consistent state and national estimates of the amounts expended by travelers, as well as of the payroll and employment generated by such expenditures and the state and local taxes paid as a consequence. Further refinements in economic impact studies are continuing.

Motivations

Market researchers are continually trying to find out what motivates people to travel. In this search, they found that demographics provided some clues, but more information was needed, especially when it was discovered that people of quite different demographic characteristics often took the same trips.

This continuing search for better traveler information has led to surveying people to find the activities they like to engage in, the things they give priority to, their opinions of themselves and others, and basic demographics. This cluster of measures has come to be known as psychographics,[19] applied in the hope of gaining greater insight into why people travel.

For example, market researcher Edward Mayo[20] studied the psychographic characteristics of visitors to twenty-four national parks dispersed throughout the United States. His method used a questionnaire of eighty-five psychographic statements dealing with topics such as daily activities, interests, opinions, and attitudes toward various aspects of a vacation, types of destinations, and overall consumption behavior. His study revealed that only two significant demographic factors were related to their attractiveness rating of the parks—higher education and higher income. Such factors as sex, age, type or location of residence, occupation, and family size were not significantly related. However, out of the eighty-five psychographic or life-style statements tested, eighteen were related to attractiveness ratings. This discovery led Mayo to categorize tourists according to seven types—the adventurer, the planner, the impulse decision maker, the action-oriented person, the outdoorsman, the escapist, and the self-designated opinion leader.

Taking a slightly different approach, Stanley C. Plog categorized all travelers according to psychographic segments distributed along a spectrum extending, at one pole, from the *psychocentric* (inhibited, nonadventurous travelers) to the *allocentric* traveler demanding change and adventure. As one might expect, the bulk of travelers fit into the intermediate area, which Plog defined as *mid-centric*.[21]

Further study by Plog identified five basic motivations for leisure travel, with the following distribution:

| | |
|---|---|
| Life is too short | 35% |
| Add interest to life | 30% |
| Need to unwind/relax | 29% |
| Ego support (service from others) | 4% |
| Sense of self-discovery | 4% |

## Benefits

Market specialists now believe that benefits, not what products *are* but what they *will do for us*, are key measures of consumer behavior. One study in the United States that analyzed the benefits accrued by travelers to several semitropical destinations revealed that scenic beauty, pleasant attitudes of "natives," and suitable accommodations were of "great importance," whereas golfing and tennis were of "little importance."[22]

## Values and Life-styles

SRI International has created a value and life-style (VALS) model for categorizing Americans, which has been applied to the analysis and marketing of tourism.[23] It divides the population into nine life-styles or types, which are grouped into four categories based on each group's self-image, aspirations, values and beliefs, and the products it uses. The four categories and nine life-styles are:

> Need-driven groups
>   survivor life-style
>   sustainer life-style
> Outer-directed groups
>   belonger life-style
>   emulator life-style
>   achiever life-style
> Inner-directed groups
>   I-am-me life-styles
>   experiential life-styles
>   socially conscious life-styles
> Combined outer- and inner-directed group
>   integrated life-style

When the state of Pennsylvania applied this typology to a survey of its tourists in 1984, it obtained the results shown in Table 3-1.[24]

## Segmentation

As noted earlier in this chapter, only recently have designers and developers of tourism recognized that all tourists are not alike, a phenomenon that behaviorists call "market

**Table 3-1. Trips to Pennsylvania by VALS group, 1984.**

| Group | All Trips % | Business Trips % | Nonbusiness Trips % |
|---|---|---|---|
| Survivors | 2.1 | 1.7 | 2.6 |
| Sustainers | 1.7 | — | 2.2 |
| Belongers | 35.6 | 15.5 | 40.8 |
| Emulators | 5.9 | — | 7.5 |
| Achievers | 36.6 | 43.1 | 31.1 |
| I-am-mes | 0.6 | 1.7 | 0.4 |
| Experientials | 2.0 | 3.4 | 1.8 |
| Societally con | 17.8 | 34.5 | 13.6 |

segmentation." Daniel J. Stynes indicates that present studies in recreation and tourism "must generally be characterized as experimental and introductory. Many investigators lack basic grounding in marketing, and most have limited experience with clustering techniques."[25] But even at this presently rudimentary level, segmentation has meaning to the designer and developer as well as to the marketer. Segmentation suggests that care is required in the use of national, state, or provincial statistics for the design of specific sites. For example, a state survey may reveal that winter sports are on the bottom of participation lists. However, the market segment represented by winter sports enthusiasts may constitute from one-half to all of the potential visitors to a winter sports complex. Canadian Minister of Tourism Tom McMillan states:

> The days when tourism in North America was synonymous with auto touring have been replaced by highly competitive, highly segmented tourism markets demanding a melange of brightly packaged experiences from special resorts to sports and fitness to theme tours to wilderness adventure.[26]

Plog identifies five factors influencing segmentation of the travel market: travel motives, quality of product, level of customer service, price, trade-offs, or mixtures of all these factors.[27]

Studies of those who take package tours (purchasing transportation, accommodations, meals, and sightseeing as a unit in advance of

Festivals and events, such as the New Orleans Mardi Gras, are very attractive to many tourists. (Photo courtesy Louisiana Tourist Development Commission)

For others, the solitude of places like the Gulf Islands National Seashore is important. (Photo: Richard Frear, courtesy National Park Service)

travel) show that such tours are taken most frequently for recreation, entertainment, and sightseeing, and are taken by mid-scale, better-educated couples without children, as compared with travelers in general. Domestic tours are shorter, more business-oriented, less apt to include married couples, and make use of ground transportation modes to a larger extent than do foreign tours.[28]

A study of vacationers in Michigan used factor analysis to determine segments. Six were identified: the young sports type, the outdoorsman/hunter type, the resort type, the sightseer type, and the nightlife activities type.[29]

Without doubt, researchers will devise other approaches in the future to gain better insight into traveler characteristics. While most of this research is tailored to marketing and promotional efforts, designers can achieve much greater understanding of the users of designed environments through study of these approaches. Bringing researchers of behavior, sociology, and psychology into the design process should greatly enhance the success of the final product.

## PUBLIC INVOLVEMENT

Apart from design professionals—architects, landscape architects, engineers, sculptors—the public can influence tourism design and development. Design has become democratized and public groups have become more articulate, challenging the purported omniscience of technologists and designers. As these groups have organized themselves according to special interests (youth groups, hotel managers, park managers, conservationists, economic developers, and so forth), the role of the politician has become more complicated, slowing the process of decision making but, perhaps, improving it.

For example, a study of public involvement in the development of tourism in two British Columbia, Canada, cities demonstrates increasing public involvement.[30] The study included the following specific guidelines: (1) tourism development should relate to overall development priorities identified by residents;

(2) promotion should be subject to local endorsement; (3) life-styles of native populations should be respected; (4) broad local support should be obtained for all tourist events and activities; and (5) plans for the growth of tourism should include steps to mitigate any negative impact of such growth.

Lane L. Marshall identified four participant groups that have increasing influence on design decisions: governments, major corporations, nonprofit foundations, and special interest groups.[31] Relative to the private sector, governments have demonstrated their inability to build and manage many tourist services. Future governments, especially in North America, are likely to emphasize incentives for private enterprise rather than direct intervention. More corporations are looking beyond the bottom line of profit-and-loss statements and accepting responsible social roles. Philanthropy will have an increasing influence on the design and development of tourism. The involvement of U.S. foundations in redesigning and restoring heritage in cities already has had an important influence.

The energies of special interest groups are difficult to harness, yet such groups pull increasing weight in democratic societies. Marshall identifies three problems of citizen involvement: crisis and reactive rather than proactive, noise (only the most vocal are heard), and belated involvement in the decision-making process.[32]

Designers have the greatest ability and opportunity to exercise a catalytic role in bringing these public groups together. Through a neutral and objective posture, they could stimulate the involvement of all major interests *throughout* the decision-making process.

This new role for designers demands attitudinal and functional changes on the part of public groups as well. They must be willing to participate in open-minded and meaningful dialogue, and, to this end, must have full opportunity for expression. Designers must break from their traditional job-contracting roles to become leaders, coordinators, and facilitators. Much progress in innovative design has already resulted from this reconceived function, and to ignore it is very possibly to inhibit adaptive change. In San Antonio, for example, architect O'Neil Ford's concept for "retaining much of the ambience of the original neighborhood" went unheeded during development of the Hemisfair in 1968. After almost two decades, during which the site languished in disrepair and misuse, new plans are finally being considered.[33]

## PUBLIC AGENCIES AND DEVELOPMENT

In a market economy country such as the United States, it might appear that laissez-faire would disallow business regulation, especially regarding something as individual as design. To the contrary, many cities now have enacted regulations that impose design controls on themselves. A study by Partners for Livable Places, a nonprofit facilitator of improved communities, lists examples of several types of controls important to tourism. The following examples are drawn from their publication *Negotiating for Amenities*.[34]

### Plazas and Streetscapes

Developers of urban tourist destinations have welcomed the recent revitalization of downtown areas. To facilitate long-awaited change, urban legislators have constructed legal foundations that underline and regulate new design.

San Francisco included two innovative design policies in its master plan of 1981. The first aims to conserve the traditional relationship between street and building, stipulating that new construction reflect the diversity and close relationship between buildings and frontage that had existed in the past. The second requires that downtown streetscapes have human scale and interest. For example, buildings must have "active ground floor uses and interesting architectural features within the limits of peripheral vision."[35] Spaces should include stores and services that are of interest to pedestrians. "Attention to surface treatment and street landscaping and furniture should

contribute to maintaining a positive environment. . . . Sculpture and fountains can transform undistinguished areas into places of excitement and interest."[36] These proposals are in tune with tourist interests for commercial centers. "Intimate, small scale, pedestrian oriented streets containing clusters of restaurants, shops and other retail uses are important attributes of the downtown."[37]

A Miami city ordinance boldly advocates, rather than restricts, flashy and conspicuous signs in certain areas around plazas and other spaces linking enclosed malls to the outdoor pedestrian environment. Although such signs are prohibited in other zones, the attempt to create an area of bright lights and excitement appeals to both visitors and residents.

New York has already stimulated downtown plazas with bonus floor-area provisions. Now, another policy seeks to enhance the visitor's value of such places with bonuses based on street furniture and other amenities desired by visitors to the downtown. Washington, D.C., is also considering the advantages to builders and pedestrians alike of bonus allowances for downtown plaza development.

### Historic Redevelopment

Many cities in the United States and elsewhere have enacted ordinances to stimulate and regulate historic redevelopment, a very important aspect of destination development.

Toronto's guidelines for protecting the historic value of its downtown have two purposes: to ensure that existing buildings of historic significance or architectural merit are retained and to ensure that new buildings are integrated with existing structures. These guidelines denounce the practice of "lifting buildings from their original sites and towing them away to historical graveyards." Adaptive reuse, the incorporation of new functions in older sites and buildings, and sensitive integration of old and new are encouraged.

Cities that are tourism destinations, such as Charleston, South Carolina, have enacted ordinances to cope with pressures from increased visitors and from heritage protectionists. Two special districts with their own regulations have been declared—"old city" and "old and historic." The purposes are: to ensure that the harmonious outward appearance of historic structures is preserved for visitors and citizens; to preserve certain structures; and to integrate new building with the style, form, color, proportion, and texture of the district. The city's Board of Architectural Review has broad authority to implement the ordinances through permitting.

Pittsburgh's guidelines for Market Square also illustrate the trend toward design controls in historic redevelopment. These guidelines include concepts for landscaping, construction materials, windows and doors, colors and finishes, storefronts, signs, and lighting, as well as requirements such as safety and building codes and standards for mechanical services.

## Scenic and View Protection

For a long time it was believed that the aesthetic quality of a structure or site could not be controlled and that regulations must be concerned only with ensuring the safety and health of potential users. Today, however, the concept of public welfare has been reinterpreted to include the preservation and creation of scenic beauty.

In order to improve the cityscape, particularly the masses of new high-rise buildings downtown, Edmonton, Alberta, has enacted general "building envelope" guidelines. These provide some control over the appearance of the built environment by defining the maximum volume of space within which buildings may be designed.

San Francisco and several other large cities have established "bulk controls," which attempt to curtail the construction of large, box-like buildings devoid of architectural detail or interest. Portland, Oregon, has an overlay zone similar to a historic district, but its controls are broadened to include scenic as well as historic areas.

Cincinnati, Ohio, nestled in a predominantly hilly landscape, has enacted a hillside ordinance. This is guided by the Cincinnati Hillside Trust, which advocates mixing land uses on the hillsides to balance social, economic, historic, aesthetic, and ecological concerns. It first acquires easements, develops design guidelines, and then conveys the land to developers.

Scenic highways have been implemented through a variety of approaches, some more successful than others. Los Angeles has a scenic highway ordinance imposing a number of design and development standards within the boundaries of the highway corridor. These include controls on the landscape as well as on the size and location of signs, parking, roadway alignment, and on landscape siting and building design.

Few cities control vistas as thoroughly as does Toronto. Because views are considered public amenities for visitors and citizens alike, they are designated like landmarks. New construction cannot interfere with these public views and, in some cases, private property is considered public because of its visual appeal. Of particular interest for the design of tourism are the provisions protecting certain views of commercial, industrial, and mechanical activities, such as railway yards or printing presses.

At the opposite end of the urban-remote scale are the scenic highway designations of rural and "rustic" roads, such as the Rustic Roads Systems in Wisconsin, created by a 1973 act of the state legislature. The purpose is threefold: (1) to preserve unusual or outstanding natural or cultural roads, (2) to use them as linear parkways, and (3) to maintain their unique qualities not only through standards of upkeep but also through zoning of roadside areas. By means of specifications for qualifications, thirty-two rustic roads totaling over one hundred fifty miles had been designated by 1985.[38]

## CONCLUSIONS

All measureable characteristics of travelers must be understood by the designer and assimilated into his vocabulary. Instead of expecting all tourists to respond with equal satisfaction to a given built environment, the designer must recognize that the great variability of tourists' expectations and images will result in diverse reactions. While the designer cannot be expected to have the specialized training of the consumer behaviorist, he can benefit greatly by adding this dimension to his consultant and design team for all tourism development projects. Travel behavior research is being reported in several readily available journals.

Demographic information provides basic data about travelers, but researchers are turning increasingly to other measures, such as psychographics, benefits, or life-styles, because of their relation to traveler decisions.

Several public groups influence the design process. Governments, corporations, nonprofit foundations, and special interest groups need to be made a part of design decisions.

While a free and open market system allows freedom of expression in tourism design and development, some guidance through controls and regulations is of value. Key regulations that are gaining acceptance include those for plazas and streetscapes, historic redevelopment, and scenic and view protection.

The lesson to be learned is that the designer must become versed in the behavior, attitudes, and influences of many public groups. Assistance can be found not only in studies of consumer behavior and tourism markets, but also in studies that integrate behavior and design.[39] David Lowenthal states, "to be effective, therefore, planning and design should be grounded on intimate knowledge of the ways people think and feel about environment; this calls for substantial familiarity with psychology and philosophy, with art and anthropology."[40] To the designer's art, creativity, and leadership must be added greater sensitivity to people as observers and users of the designed environment.

# 4/

# Attractions: First Power

Washington, D.C., as a seat of American government and shrines, brings thousands of visitors to carry on professional, political, and business activities. Houston, as a trade center, lures thousands of visitors to conduct business and participate in conferences and conventions. The unique land characteristics of Hawaii Volcanoes National Park make it one of the most popular parks in the world despite the 2,600 miles of ocean that separate it from the United States mainland. The appealing forests and waters of a youth camp encourage young people to take part in outdoor experiences. The restored vibrant section of a city, such as the French Quarter of New Orleans, causes thousands of visitors to immerse themselves in history during the day and raucous excitement at night. Despite their diversity, these places have in common an appeal that is not incidental to highway location. All are targets for purposeful, rather than haphazard, trips. Because of the pull they exert on the traveler, all can be classified by the generic term *attractions*, a label that is not only appropriate, but frees the designer from the limitations of more restrictive labels, such as *parks* or *resorts*.

Without developed attractions tourism as we now know it could not exist; there would be little need for transportation, facilities, services, and information systems. The principle of attraction is so important that it deserves deeper examination by designers, especially as the growth and expansion of present environments are considered.

## AN ANCIENT CONCEPT

Throughout time man has had a burning desire to experience the exotic, and just as quickly as means were made available to him he did so. The ancient Greeks traveled within their own land and to nearby countries for trade, cultural enrichment, and better health (the local spas were well equipped with physical-fitness programs). The Romans were lured by the sea, the countryside, and the cosmopolitan pleasures offered by the metropolis, including theater and gladiators' combat. Then as now shrines, religious festivals, and athletic competitions were prominent attractions.

Through the ages educational values have been attached to travel. In Shakespeare's *Two Gentlemen of Verona* they are well promoted.

Buffalo National River. (Photo: Kenneth L. Smith, courtesy National Park Service)

*Panthino:* Some to the wars, to try their
    fortune there;
Some to discover Islands far away;
Some to the studious Universities;
For any, or for all of these exercises
He said, that Proteus your son was meet,
And did request me to importune you
To let him spend his time no more at home,
Which would be great impeachment to his
    age,
In having known no travel in his youth.

*Antonio:* Nor need'st thou much importune
    me to that
Whereon this month I have been hamering.
I have consider'd well, his loss of time
And how he cannot be a perfect man,
Not being tryed and tutor'd in the world:
Experience is by industry achieved
And perfected by the swift course of time.[1]

In the eighteenth and nineteenth centuries no English student of quality completed his education without taking the Grand Tour. Undoubtedly the first package tour in history, this extensive trip included the highlights of France, Switzerland, Italy, Germany, and the Low Countries. The beauty of foreign lands profoundly influenced the literature of Rousseau, Shelley, Byron, and Ruskin, and the paintings of Turner. In this period, landscape art was doing an equally powerful job of opening the eyes of masses to the pleasures of foreign travel.

## TRAVEL, WORLDWIDE

Today travel exceeds even military spending as a major item of world trade. It has personal, social, and environmental importance as well as economic significance. Spain, because of

For people of ancient Greece and Rome, cultural and trade attractions stimulated much travel. (Photo of the Irodus Atticus Theatre courtesy Union News Photo, Athens, Greece)

Medieval Toledo, the capital of Spain in 1085 and now a Spanish national monument, is a major attraction for tourists. Note the Moorish and Gothic architecture.

Toledo, El Escorial, Segovia, Madrid, the Mediterranean coast, and the northern mountains, has more foreign tourists annually than residents. Other countries cope with a similar situation, adjusting to millions of foreigners. Developed countries seek to maintain and increase present levels of tourism while undeveloped countries see tourism as a potential salvation to economic woes. Whatever the motivations, international travel continues to grow.

Because the United States sends many more travelers to foreign destinations than it receives, there has not been pressure to enhance the quality of land design and management for foreigners. This need for designs that are sensitive to the requirements of foreign travelers is one of the greatest challenges to design professions in the United States today.

## TRAVEL, AMERICAN

Pleasure travel has been a dominant activity for all walks of life in the United States, even during the peak of Puritanism. Indeed, nineteenth-century clergymen could be counted among the ranks of pleasure travelers. As described by Foster Rhea Dulles:

> The Reverend John A. Clark of St. Andrew's Church in Philadelphia, who went abroad in 1840, suggests the vogue for ministerial travel when he speaks of finding aboard his ship a "pleasant, sober, clerical group." He raised a question, however, in his rambling and discursive Glimpses of the Old World. Clark was afraid that many of the clergymen whom he met in Europe had left their charges "under the pretext of enfeebled health" and actually had no more reason for going than "a desire to enjoy the pleasures" of the trip.[2]

The United States was born out of travel, and extending the frontier was of greater importance than stability, security, and tradition. Many of the forces important to pleasure travel can be read into Turner's description of the American frontier: "In spite of environment, and in spite of custom, each frontier did indeed furnish a new field of opportunity, a gate of escape from the bondage of the past; and freshness, and confidence, and scorn of older society, impatience of its restraints and the ideals, and indifference to its lessons, have accompanied the frontier."[3]

## ATTRACTION CONSTANTS

An examination of two centuries of tourism shows that many present activities are similar to those of yesterday, although some have changed or disappeared. Early accounts reveal the popularity of such then-illegal pastimes as "dice, cards, quoits, bowls, ninepins . . . Shuffle Board."[4] Good food, wine, and whiskey were accompaniments to many recreations throughout the history of America. Strolling, people-watching, attending concerts, and using "gouff clubs" were urban pastimes of the early 1700s, as were hunting, fishing, country fairs, target practice, pleasure boating, ice carnivals, skating, hockey, horse racing and other attractions requiring travel.[5]

Scenic excursions from town to town, probably the beginnings of our present "pleasure drives," were common two centuries ago. Cockfighting was a popular sport in New England and the South. Even the modern zoo had its counterpart as early as 1733, with camels, lions, polar bears, monkeys, and elephants on display.

The names may have persisted for some activities, but their functions are now expressed in different ways. Health spas have all but abandoned the mineral water cures that were famous at the turn of the century, incorporating instead a variety of health, wellness, fitness and weight-loss facilities and programs. Fishing, once simply a matter of angling, now includes the use of plane-to-boat communications and sonar to spot fishing beds. Vacation homes, previously restricted to personally owned cottages, now include condominiums in high-rise buildings or row houses as well as time-sharing options. Ship travel, formerly a class means of transoceanic transportation, is now dominated by an elaborate floating resort concept, with on-deck recreations and epicurean delights.

For the designer, perhaps the most important changes have been the proliferation of activities and the broadening of clientele. A simple activity such as camping has myriad offshoots, including wilderness camping, backpack camping, boat camping, tent camping, and recreational vehicle camping. Golfing is no longer the exclusive sport of the wealthy. Sightseers include a wide range of individuals, from the college-student hitchhiker to the multimillionaire with his private island on the opposite side of the earth. "What had once been largely restricted to the genteel members of society had become the property of the people as a whole."[6]

This historical review shows the change in use of attractions and helps demonstrate that most change involves the manner in which activities take place. The only limits are those of imagination and creativity, which are largely the responsibility of designers. And throughout the history of tourism the land and the landscape have played a dominant role.

## ATTRACTIONS RELOCATED

Because of changes in transportation technology more of today's attractions are to be found in mass complexes at travel nodes rather than scattered along roadsides. Variations in the placement of attractions are of special significance to designers and planners.

A major change in the location of attractions came with steamboat and railway travel in the late 1800s. For the first time attractions were clustered at travel termini and exchange points. In the Great Lakes region, for example, resorts with Victorian grandeur, promenades and all, flourished at port cities and points where rail lines touched beautiful lakes and lumber towns. The resort attractions were tightly grouped about the hotel, and guests strayed only as far as horse, carriage, or canoe would allow.

The automobile age initiated another major change, enabling travelers to reach thousands more attractions along roadside sites rather than merely at steamboat and railway termini. Salesmen had access to rural areas and small towns, and pleasure travelers could reach more parks, mountains, and beaches. The proliferation of highways and the comparatively slow speed of automobiles fostered hordes of roadside attractions, such as snake farms,

Petoskey, Michigan, a resort destination on the shores of Lake Michigan, as it was in 1882 during the heyday of railroad and steamboat tourism. (Photo courtesy Chicago, Grand Rapids & Indiana Railroad)

gorges, waterfalls, and shops filled with trinkets and curios.

While the automobile era fostered an explosion in mobility, which allowed penetration into untouched areas, the modern expressway and jet travel returned us to a tighter clustering of attractions. Place, the essential characteristic of an attraction, has now become far more important than in the days of shoepack and donkey. "The history of tourism clearly indicates that the environment of places has contributed to the birth and progress of tourism."[7]

## ATTRACTIONS CLASSIFIED

The abundance and diversity of travel attractions seem to defy description and certainly complicate their design. People travel world-wide to shop in department stores, to participate in international conferences, to do business with multinational firms, to visit shrines, to view contemporary and historic gardens, and to participate in cultural events. The National Council of Travel Attractions (The Travel Industry Association of America) assigned 181 key attractions of the United States to four groups: natural, historical and cultural, professional and technical, and theme parks.[8] The Texas Tourist Development Agency monitors attendance at eight types of attractions: museums, privately held attractions, U.S. Department of Interior sites, city visitor centers, state parks, U.S. Corps of Engineers lakes, state tourist bureaus, and national forests.

In consulting work and in teaching tourism

design and planning, it has been useful to divide all activities into two general classes—*touring circuit* and *longer-stay* (table 4-1). By "touring circuit" is meant those activities on a tour. Because tourists are flowing through an area, attractions require resources, design, and operations for successive groups of tourists that visit throughout a single day. Travelers will visit more than one location in the period between leaving home and returning. Categories of typical activities are listed in the table.

### Table 4-1. Classification of travel activities

**Touring Circuit Activities Categories**
Driving for pleasure, sightseeing
Visiting outstanding natural areas: parks, forests, scenery
Travel camping: tent, trailer, RV
Water touring: boating, cruising, rafting
Visiting friends/relatives, including duty travel
Visiting universities, factories, processing plants, science facilities
Visiting national, state shrines, pilgrimages, gardens
Visiting places noted for food, entertainment
Visiting historic, archaeological sites, buildings, museums
Visiting places important for ethnic foods, costumes, arts, drama
Visiting shopping areas
Visiting art, craft, gift, legendary places

**Longer-Stay Activities Categories**
Vacationing at resorts (food, lodging, fitness, recreation)
Vacationing at camp sites—parks, forest areas
Vacationing at hunting, fishing, other sports destinations
Participating in programs at organization camps
Visiting personal vacation homes
Participating in festivals, events, pilgrimages
Participating in conferences, conventions—professional-business
Vacationing at gaming centers—gambling, racing entertainment
Visiting major sports arenas—domes, coliseums
Visiting major trade centers—professional-business
Visiting science-technology centers—professional-business
Vacationing at theme parks

On the other hand, activities for "longer-stay" use require resources, design, and operations for groups of people staying for more than a brief visit. For example, a historic site can be toured in a relatively short time, perhaps an hour or so. However, travelers who use vacation homes, stay in resorts, or attend conferences, stay in one part of a destination zone for a longer time. A resort visitor can fish, boat, or swim in one general area day after day, whereas a touring-circuit traveler will attend an outdoor drama but once.

Table 4-2 merely restates these categories of activities in terms of the kinds of attraction places needed to support them. This list helps the designer recognize the difference between attraction objectives for these two major classes of markets.

While these attractions may seem to have little in common, even within a single category, some design concerns are threaded through all. Frequently attractions are united by a common geographic area, even though they function differently. New England's "roadside scenic areas," "outstanding natural areas," and "historic buildings and sites" are frequently linked together on visitor tours.

### Table 4-2. Classification of attractions

| Touring Circuit Attractions | Longer-stay Attractions |
|---|---|
| Roadside scenic areas | Resorts |
| Outstanding natural areas | Camping areas |
| Camping areas | Hunting/water sports areas |
| Water touring areas | Organization camp areas |
| Homes: friends/relatives | Vacation home complexes |
| Unusual institutions | Festival, event places |
| Shrines, cultural places | Convention, meeting places |
| Food, entertainment places | Gaming centers |
| Historic buildings, sites | Sports arenas, complexes |
| Ethnic areas | Trade centers |
| Shopping areas | Science/technology centers |
| Crafts, lore places | Theme parks |

One category of tourism, *touring circuits*, includes visiting several attractions on a tour. (Photo of Mackinac Bridge courtesy Michigan Tourist Council)

In another category of tourism, *longer-stay*, the tourist focuses on one area, such as the Little Dix Bay Resort in the British Virgin Islands. (Photo courtesy Rockresorts)

Winter and summer "resorts," "camping areas," and "fishing, hunting areas" are also located nearby. This suggests the need for collaboration, or at least cooperation, among the designers of separate attractions, although it does not mean that each attraction should lose its individuality. Certainly, the amount of time travelers budget for visits to attractions has much to do with their design. Developers of motor coach tours usually cannot include theme parks in their itineraries because they take too much time. Short-term attractions require quick and easy circulation, but focused attractions can be designed for more casual, exploratory use.

Because economic goals are so strong, the greater the aggregation of both touring circuit and longer-stay attractions, the better. Groupings provide business support for the services desired by travelers, such as hotels, food, and entertainment, but they also trigger concern over saturation and the environmental consequences of too many visitors.

## ATTRACTION COMMONALITY

For the designer, this complicated mass of attractions is baffling. On the surface no consistency is apparent. How could Six Flags Over Texas and Great Smoky Mountains National Park share common factors? If we are to deal with attractions as physical entities, however, we must know more about the characteristics that they hold in common. Recognition of six common factors is important for revising or establishing new attractions.

### Easy Comprehensibility

Designers and developers of attractions must ensure that attractions are easily and readily understood by those who use them. Every attraction should provide the user with information or perhaps skill for fullest participation. For example, in sports, many resort areas offer instruction in marksmanship, swimming, golf, waterskiing, winter skiing, fishing, or hunting. Many national parks are staffed by professional nature interpreters who tell of the area's

unique flora and fauna. Historic, archaeologic, and other heritage sites and restorations are not only labeled with descriptive information but are interpreted by guides, taped narrations, and colorful displays. If the visitor cannot understand the attraction, he loses interest, and it ceases to be an attraction.

The designer must exercise constraint so that the mechanisms that foster communication between visitor and site do not overwhelm the visitor. Sometimes visitor centers, exhibits, and signs demonstrate by their sheer mass and number that developers and designers can go too far—the original attraction function is overpowered. There is a delicate balance between allowing the visitor to gain adventure from the attraction and overwhelming the visitor with information.

### Basis in Environment

The environmental foundation for an attraction has many important implications. Even if the Sphinx were removed to the Smithsonian Institution, its roots would still be in the Sahara. Every attraction has place, both by physical location and by association. For all attractions, that association is important, but for some, it assumes an especially strong significance. It is doubtful, for example, that husbands and wives ever forget the place of their

Attractions, in order to function properly, must be fully comprehended by the visitor. (Photo of the Golden Gate National Recreation Area: Richard Frear, courtesy National Park Service)

honeymoon. "Love of one another is linked to love of place."[9]

The Garden of the Gods is at the base of the Rockies near Colorado Springs, and no amount of mental exertion could place it conceptually in Times Square. Any attraction is swept up in its environmental setting, and this makes it subject to its native climate, other natural influences, and, above all, the man-made influences surrounding it. A transplanted London Bridge remains integrally related to London even though it has been relocated to Arizona. Even siteless attractions, such as gambling, parades, and pageants, occur in some kind of setting. Therefore, in the design of attractions, the implications of locational environment are important.

> In an age of anonymity, it is important to seek out and preserve qualities which distinguish one place from another. Too often the inherent amenities and natural features which all places possess are sacrificed for the sake of economy or convenience, resulting in a loss of identity.[10]

Both environmental assets and constraints are important to future design and development of tourism. An abundance and high quality of surface water, vegetative cover, wildlife, and land relief (mountains), as well as a climate favorable to outdoor recreation are important resources upon which tourism may be developed. Polluted water, cold water (short season), deserts, sparse wildlife, and climates neither cold enough for winter sports nor warm enough for relief from northern climates have limited tourism potential. Natural assets are further enhanced for tourism development where access is available and a service city is nearby.

In the last decade, markets interested in history and cultural backgrounds have increased greatly. This demand factor has brought historic sites and buildings, ethnic arts and crafts, festivals, shrines, and man-made spectacles (for example, manufacturing plants) into the category of resources for tourism development.

The many natural and cultural resources therefore form the foundation upon which

Attractions are anchored to their environment. (Photo of the Garden of the Gods in Colorado, courtesy Parks and Recreation Department, Colorado Springs)

tourism development can be considered. It must be emphasized, however, that these resources are specific to locations and are not equally distributed over a single region or country.

> In the course of time the landscape, whether that of a large region like a country or of a small locality like a market town, acquires its specific *genius loci*, its culture- and history-conditioned character which commonly reflects not only on the work and the aspirations of the society at present in occupancy but also that of its precursors in the area.[11]

## Owner Control

An added ingredient for the success of any attraction is that of effective ownership and management. All attractions belong to someone—individual or group, public or private.

All attractions are managed according to the owners' policies, which vary greatly. (Photo of Ococe Lake, courtesy Tennessee Valley Authority)

They are therefore developed according to specific policies and practices: commercial owners implement designs that increase profits; government owners implement designs that fulfill social objectives.

Several countries have traditionally looked toward government for the development of attractions that are based primarily on natural resources. Many believe that only governments can supply wholesome and worthwhile attractions. In recent years, however, the Disneylands and Williamsburgs have demonstrated that social values can be upheld by attractions designed and managed by the private sector.

The designer can perform a critical catalytic role in balancing ownership policies with the needs of visitors. For example, an owner-developer of a resort hotel complex may wish to take full advantage of a linkage with a beautiful beach and water resource. He may consider a site directly on the beach to be optimal. However, the designer may emphasize the finite quantity of beachfront and favor clusters of structures that allow open spaces between

them to maximize views and access to buildings farther back from the beach. It is the designer's role to help developers reach their objectives and at the same time protect both the visitor's interests and the environmental assets. Throughout the process, designers can provide more satisfying and attractive developments, no matter what ownership policies prevail.

Magnetism

By definition an attraction is magnetic. It must draw people. The concept that an attraction is defined by its pulling power is antithetical to the beliefs of many for whom an attraction comes into being merely by the owner's declaration and construction. The true test of being is pulling power.

The concept of magnetism (pull) has two corollaries that are of concern to the designer. First, magnetism exists in the eyes of the visitor, and each visitor has unique interests and preferences (see Chapter 4). Second, magnetism is also a quality of the design, development, and managerial operation of an attraction. Designers can create magnetic attractions from given environmental assets.

Again, emphasis must be placed on the need for an attraction to meet the needs of a specific market segment or several segments at one time. When the designer brings market interest and resource potential together to create an attraction, greater success is assured.

Capacity to Satisfy

Another corollary of pulling power is visitor satisfaction. A successful attraction is rewarding to the participants, and attendance figures alone do not reveal the depth of user satisfaction. This is the major challenge in designing and establishing attractions. If the visitor leaves feeling disappointed, uninterested, or even defrauded, the attraction may have suc-

By definition, attractions must be magnetic, providing a pull upon markets. (Photo of the Texas Prison Rodeo courtesy Texas State Department of Highways and Public Transportation)

The ultimate test of an attraction is its ability to provide satisfaction to visitors. (Photo of the Sam Rayburn Reservoir courtesy Texas State Department of Highways and Public Transportation)

Even natural features require creative development to become an attraction. (Photo of Yosemite Falls: C. W. Stoughton, courtesy National Park Service)

ceeded in attracting but not in carrying out its complete function. If a designer is to produce successful attractions, his designs must elicit user satisfaction.

### Result of Man's Creation

Every attraction today is created. This statement may seem fatuous, especially in the face of such natural wonders as the Grand Canyon, Yosemite Falls, and the Giant Redwoods. Nevertheless, in the context of modern tourism, even the most compelling places do not become true attractions until they are provided with access, lookout points, parking areas, interpretation programs, and linkages with service centers.

One can think of this concept in the negative as well. Our ability to alter the environment is so facile today that choosing *not* to change a natural feature is itself an act of creation. However, seldom can an attraction be merely a locked-up resource. Fires, earthquakes, floods, insects, and disease change or destroy natural features, and management control must be exercised even to "preserve" them.

Along with the power to create attractions must come the responsibility to protect resources. These are two sides of the same coin. One can protect fragile sites by limiting structural development and restricting visitor use. Meanwhile, one can develop "hardened" sites nearby for facilities and services.

### AUTHENTICITY

For some, the idea of *designed, created,* and *developed* attractions may smack of arrogance or even fraud. Travelers around the globe complain about gross misrepresentations. There are instances where jewelry, crafts, dances, and costumes are identified as having genuine ethnic origins, but turn out to be fakes. Festivals are sometimes falsely advertised as based in historical fact. "Tourism has been accused of being 'culturally arrogant' for manipulating the traditions and customs of people to make tourist experiences more interesting and satisfying."[12]

But how can one define a "true" experience? What is now one of Hawaii's greatest appeals, its fluid patois in song, came not so much from the native Polynesians as from New York's "Tin Pan Alley" of the early 1900s. Using this nonnative genre, composers wrought an amalgam of the special sights, sounds, smells, and language of Hawaii that evokes, for visitors, heartfelt emotions never possible from the nonmelodic grunts of pure Polynesian origin. Who would say that the very particular and pleasurable feelings millions of visitors associate with Hawaiiana are false?

When a developer reconstructed old Fort Michilimackinac in northern Michigan in the 1960s, he faced a major decision regarding authenticity. The original structures, erected in 1763 and long rotted away, had been built on the ground or on local stone rubble. The developer, Dr. Eugene Peterson, made the policy decision that all the 1763 structures would be built on concrete faced with the old stone. This would present the buildings in their true setting but the $3 million invested would not have to be replaced in a few years. Millions of future visitors will appreciate this policy decision.

Historic reuse is an attempt to have the best of both worlds—the essence of an earlier era without the high cost of maintaining a museum. Pierre Berton comments about Canada's Main Street Program: "It's no use preserving a building unless a use can be found for it. It's no use preserving a streetscape if it is not economically viable."[13] In order for these buildings to function as travel attractions, new air conditioning, heating, plumbing, and electrical systems must be incorporated. All these modifications test the skill of designers, who must ensure that the spirit and drama of the "real" thing is not spoiled.

The issue of authenticity of tourist attractions relates to the ethics of promotion. If buildings and sites are purported to be something they are not, the public may be disappointed and even angry. Travelers today are more sophisticated than many developers and promoters realize. It is important to be careful when using descriptors such as "the original,"

"the real thing," "the exact place where this event took place," or "handmade." Honesty in advertising demands that such phrases as "a replication," "near the place of an event," or "manufactured" be used where appropriate. The difference between a documentation and a drama needs to be explicit. Drama is an art form and can be an important attraction adjunct.

Restored historic buildings often suffer from inappropriate landscapes. While mass use may necessitate such features as hard surfaces for walks, the designer can often utilize period designs and materials to minimize wear and tear. Research into the landscape materials of a period is as important as the study of architectural detailing.

## TRIPARTITE ATTRACTION CONCEPT

The study of tourist attractions in the context of visitors and settings reveals elements and relationships that may be useful in the design of future attractions. The concept of an attraction being composed of three important functional parts provides a useful means of examining these elements and their relationships (fig. 4-1).

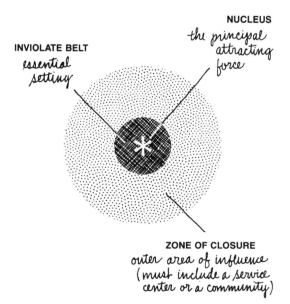

4-1. *Tripartite attraction design.* All three zones —nucleus, inviolate belt, and zone of closure— require special design attention.

## The Nucleus

The prime element of an attraction, its raison d'être, is the *nucleus*. For a waterfall, the nucleus is the falling water; for a mountain, it is the peak; for an area rich in historical significance, it is the landscape or building. In the design of attractions the nucleus must be of the type and quality to match or surpass the images held by tourists.

If the nucleus is a fragile or rare resource extreme care must be taken in designing it for visitors, especially for large numbers. The public may be held at the edge of a prime resource feature and allowed to experience it vicariously through interpretive lectures, presentations, pageantry, simulation, exhibits, overlooks, or specially designed transportation for sightseeing. These methods prevent physical contact that may be environmentally damaging.

## The Inviolate Belt

The function of attractions equally depends on the setting, or *inviolate belt*. The visitor can reach a feature (nucleus) only by passing through some buffer space, which may be small, large, short, long, brief, or of extended duration. Physio-psychological conditioning is the function of this space. It is the frame for the feature.

A person's mind set or anticipation of an attraction has much to do with his reception and approval when the nucleus is reached. Without a doubt, the inviolate belt has a much more powerful function than has been previously attributed to it. No nucleus can be without it. It requires special sensitivity and creativity on the part of the designer.

This inviolate belt can be very difficult to incorporate into the overall design of an attraction. Others own properties surrounding the nucleus, and they often have quite different land-use purposes and policies. For example, a historic building is often surrounded by contemporary structures with no visitor functions. Every effort should be made to consider the design requirements of the inviolate belt surrounding attraction nuclei.

## The Zone of Closure

Especially important to all tourism-related firms is a third aspect of attractions, the surrounding area, or *zone of closure*. Within this zone must be found one or more service centers as well as transportation linkage between service centers and attractions. Service centers contain the business places and community services needed by the traveler—lodging, food, entertainment, car service, communications, banking, information, and retail purchases. No matter how remote the attraction, some service center must be available and accessible in order for the attraction to function.

This principle is demonstrated by the relationship between the service centers of Gatlinburg and Cherokee and the attractions of Great Smoky Mountains National Park (fig. 4-2). The National Park Service protects the several attraction nuclei and provides visitors interpretation. The nuclei are surrounded by an inviolate belt of a complementary landscape setting. The many services desired by travelers are provided in nearby cities and are linked to the park by major highway corridors.

The zone of closure concept suggests a need for greater design and jurisdictional cooperation than generally exists today. The interdependent functions of the many sites within the zone are not always clear to the numerous owners. The landscape architect could assist all owners and developers in understanding the personal benefits of applying this concept. Developers of attractions could exercise resource protection policies more effectively without having to provide services. Businesses that do provide services could become more successful by understanding the market trends of visitors to the attractions. Finally, traveler satisfaction would be enhanced by an integrated design of service centers, attractions, and transportation linkages.

## COMPLEXES

When attractions are grouped into larger complexes they thrive better than smaller, isolated ones. This principle has been fostered partly

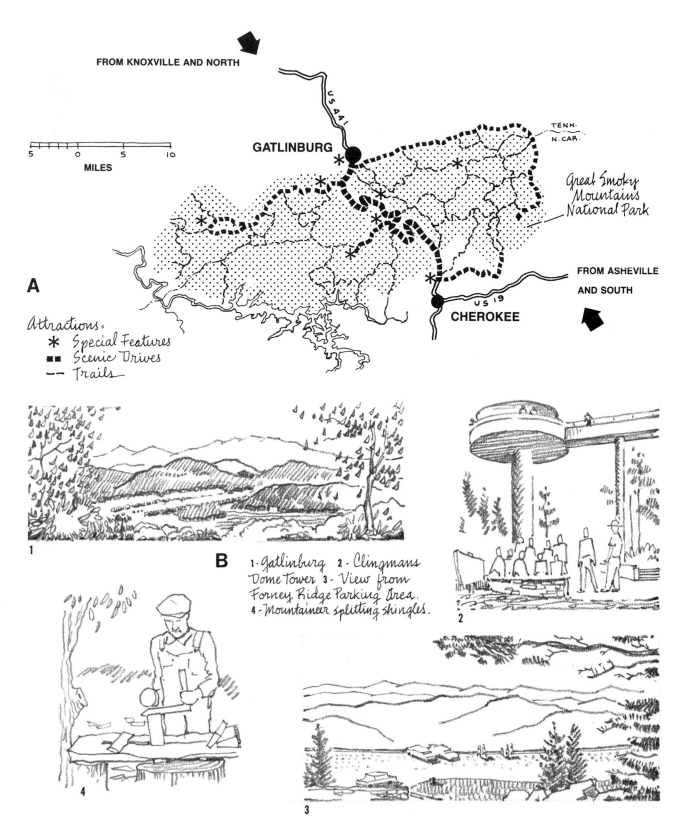

GATLINBURG

TENN.
N. CAR.

Great Smoky
Mountains
National Park

FROM ASHEVILLE
AND SOUTH

CHEROKEE

MILES

**A**

Attractions:
* Special Features
■■ Scenic Drives
-- Trails

**B** 1-Gatlinburg 2-Clingmans
Dome Tower 3-View from
Forney Ridge Parking Area.
4-Mountaineer splitting shingles.

**4-2.** *Example of attraction complex.* (A.) Map showing relationship of Gatlinburg and Cherokee service centers to the attractions within Great Smoky Mountains National Park. (B.) Sketches of a few of the major attractions.

Well-designed tourist services with height limits and other design controls, such as those in Gatlinburg, Tennessee, provide for essential needs of visitors to major attractions. (Photo: Ben Humphries, courtesy Gatlinburg Chamber of Commerce)

by the dominance of expressway and jet travel, which supported the clustering of attractions at termini. But more likely it is the result of travelers' demands for greater recreational and business opportunities at destinations. Detailed examination of natural and cultural resources can reveal a potential for larger complexes. For example, important forest, wildlife, or historic sites may be prime areas for attraction complexes with scenic, hunting, and historical themes. A study of markets could reveal the extent to which a designer can group several compatible complexes together, even those that have different owners.

Many national parks are large attraction complexes because they provide opportunities for viewing scenery, photographing natural resources, hiking, and horseback riding, as well as social activities related to the park, such as camping and visiting interpretation centers.

A major single complex is more efficiently engineered and controlled than many smaller attractions widely dispersed. The cost of water supply, sewage disposal, electrical power, and roads is reduced in a single complex as compared to several areas miles apart. Police protection, fire protection, and management control is more efficient with a more compact setting. As public park and theme park managers have experienced, it is much easier to manage crowds in a single area with one entrance than in many areas far apart.

When a study of markets and resources suggests that visitors' interests will conflict, attraction complexes should be segregated. Incompatible elements should be designed and managed independently. For example, park managers have successfully separated areas for day users from those for longer-stay users. RV users have been accorded different sites from tent campers. Historic site visitors have been separated from beach and boat users. And wilderness buffs have pursued their interests in places unoccupied by gregarious park users.

# CONCLUSIONS

A major component of the tourism system, *attractions*, has many design implications. While the total supply side of tourism exercises a pull on markets, the attractions of a destination are particularly influential in drawing visitors. With greater input from professional designers, attractions can become more effective and meaningful.

Although the idea of what constitutes an attraction has changed over the years, attractions have been with us for centuries. The mystique of distant places lures populations everywhere, while advanced technology of transportation has given travelers more opportunities to visit attractions throughout the world.

While attractions seem to be quite different from one another, they share certain characteristics that are important to designers. All attractions can be grouped into two major categories: those intended for touring-circuit use and those for longer-stay use. In addition, designers need to be aware of desirable characteristics for all attractions: well comprehended by visitors, appropriate to the environment, influenced by owners' policies and objectives, providers of a magnetic function, a source of visitor satisfaction, and created.

The designer ought to be concerned with the authenticity of an attraction. Ethics and professionalism demand not only high quality in design but also honest presentation. The designer's license is broad enough to meet the imagery and needs of visitors without violating the integrity of place.

Conceptually, designers need to think of attraction development in its broadest context. Not only is the design of the *nucleus* important, but so is that of surrounding features—the *inviolate belt* and the *zone of closure*, which should include one or more carefully developed *service centers*. Finally, more comprehensive attraction complexes are more interesting, more economical to build, and more efficiently managed than widely dispersed small ones.

The designer's role is to assist developers and managers to attract visitors and provide them with rich and satisfying experiences. An equal obligation is to use the indigenous qualities of a place with sensitivity, so that resources are protected.

# Tourism Destinations

Places that represent *here* for the local resident become *there* for visitors from another origin. The characteristics of here, if they are to become the supply side of tourism, must be designed to meet the expectations of residents and outsiders alike. Fortunately, this task is simplified by the knowledge that the majority of development for visitors is similar for residents. For example, tourists enjoy, as do residents, parks, scenic roadsides, entertainment, specialty food establishments, and streets that are clean, safe, and walkable at night.

A better term for *there* is *destination*. Tourist destinations do not originate on the marketer's desk but are the result of creative design and development schemes coupled with appealing resources that are indigenous to a place.

## DESTINATION CHARACTERISTICS

The design and development of tourist destinations could be facilitated greatly by knowing in advance the characteristics that will influence the impact of development. Alister Mathieson and Geoffrey Wall have provided the following list of key characteristics to be analyzed:

Rouen Cathedrale. (Photo courtesy French Government Tourist Office)

1. *Natural environmental features and processes.* These include topography; mountains, lakes, rivers and sea; soil, vegetation, flora and fauna; sunshine, temperature, precipitation, photosynthesis, erosion, and other environmental processes.
2. *Economic structure and economic development.* This includes the level of economic development; the diversity of the economic base; the spatial characteristics of development; patterns of investment; and the import-export characteristics of the revenue of the destination.
3. *Social structure and organization.* This category includes the demographic profile of the host population; strength of local culture; availability and quality of social amenities; patterns of social organization; women in the work-force; religious affiliations; moral conduct; levels of health and safety; perceptions, attitudes and values towards tourists; language; traditions and gastronomic practices.
4. *Political organizations.* The political structure of the host country and of particular resorts is important. Such factors as the existence of capitalist or socialist principles; planning regulation, incentives and constraints; and the roles of national, regional and local tourist organizations influence tourist impacts.

5. *Level of tourist development.* This encompasses the degree of local involvement in the tourist industry; rate of development; nature and diversity of attractions; types and quality of accommodation; entertainment and eating facilities; and the role of travel intermediaries.[1]

## DESTINATION CONCEPT

Most of the design and planning problems described earlier in this book could be solved by reconsidering destinations as a whole, that is, grouping the tripartite attraction units described in Chapter 4 together, as illustrated in figure 5-1. This procedure allows a broader perspective and stimulates greater design integration.

The "section" of figure 5-1 dramatizes the need for integrated planning and design of destinations. The travel flow begins at home and passes along water, land, or air circulation corridors. All travel modes lead the traveler to termini, predominantly located in communities, where many attractions and services are located. The point where one enters these communities from the circulation corridor is an important visual transition. First impressions influence the remaining experiences both negatively and positively. The traveler then moves on through linkage corridors to surrounding attraction clusters. Every one of these steps is a design challenge.

Figure 5-1 also includes a plan view of these functions, which may be used as a guide for analyzing and planning new destinations as well as modifying existing ones. For example, if some resources have not been developed into attraction clusters served by well-designed linkage corridors and accessible community services, there may be an opportunity to create a new destination zone. It must be emphasized, however, that destination zones originate as much from market forces as from intrinsic physical resources.

Following is a brief description of the major elements of destination zones.

1. **Attraction clusters** form the backbone of tourist destinations. After a designer thoroughly studies the resource potential of an area he may have an opportunity to develop new attraction clusters that are of interest to several market segments.

Indeed, the future success of an attraction cluster, in terms of visitor satisfaction, business success, and resource protection, rests heavily on the shoulders of design professionals. Several design scenarios are possible. The design and development may be so inept that the term *tourist attraction* becomes synonymous with *tourist trap.* Or designs may be so ordinary that the attraction fails to sustain the tourist's interest. Finally, and much more challenging and desirable, is the attraction cluster that makes outstanding use of resources and enriches visitors while supporting profitable business.

An example of an attraction cluster is illustrated in figure 5-2. On the basis of the cluster-design principle, a dramatic, interesting, and educational attraction complex could be developed in the Great Lakes timber region. Here, from 1880 through 1930, timber that was used to build the frontier cities of the Midwest was the foundation of the economy. Today, this chapter in American history is nearly forgotten, but research shows that several aspects of the area would lend themselves well to redevelopment. By incorporating a river, a harbor, and related sites that played important roles in history, a fascinating complex could be restored with the following six attractions.

*Railroad town:* Features could include a restored version of the community, with a general store, cabins, steam sawmill, blacksmith shop, and bars. Exhibits could include equipment, machinery, and processes of that era.

*Lumber camp:* Features could include a restored cabin with a smoke hole in the roof, open fire, and bunkhouses; cook's cabin; beanhole; barns, granary, and blacksmith shop; logging trails; skidding trails;

**RADIAL DISTINATION ZONE**

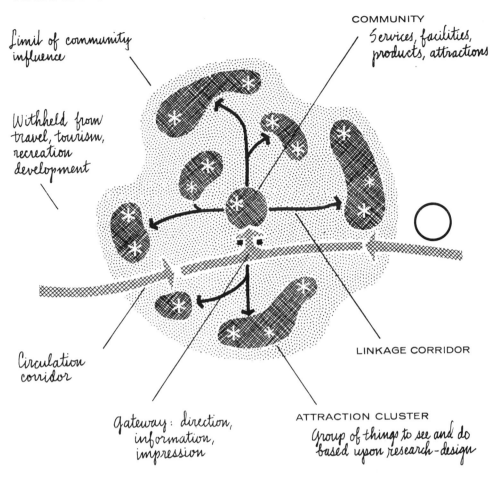

COMMUNITY
*Services, facilities, products, attractions*

*Limit of community influence*

*Withheld from travel, tourism, recreation development*

*Circulation corridor*

LINKAGE CORRIDOR

*Gateway: direction, information, impression*

ATTRACTION CLUSTER
*Group of things to see and do based upon research-design*

**Section**

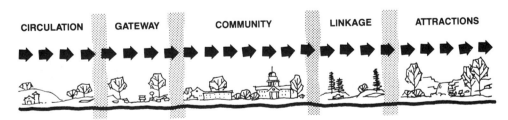

CIRCULATION    GATEWAY    COMMUNITY    LINKAGE    ATTRACTIONS

**5-1.** *Radial destination zone.* Designers can determine the potential for tourism development by analyzing resources within a reasonable radius of a city.

skidways; sleigh trails to landings; and banked logs at landings. Exhibits of tools and equipment used in the pre-railroad era, and action displays of axe cutting, cross-cut sawing, marking, skidding, sleighing and banking, could be provided.

*River driving camp:* Features could include camp tents, an outdoor cooking area, dams, piers, and a boom-company farm. Exhibits could include oxen teams, bateaux, peaveys, poles, a cook's outfit, and a blacksmith's outfit. Action displays could include use of bateaux, breaking a log jam, eating while balancing on a log, and birling.

*Sawdust town:* The possibility exists of restoring actual buildings on their original sites. Features could include bars, restaurants, and a floating night club, all of which could simulate the original interior design, exterior design, and functions. The flavor, glamor, zest, interest, and character of the lumber era would dominate. Here also would be located ample displays and sales areas for souvenirs and gifts. This grouping would offer some of the commercial and lighter aspects, such as saloons, that would be out of place in other parts of the complex.

*Sawmill:* Features could include a restored pre-1900 sawmill; pond; river storage; booms, piles, log pockets, river tugs, and lumber schooners; catchmarking sheds; tally shanties, and scaling gaps; boarding houses; refuse burner; and sorting shed. Action displays could reenact the complete process of producing lumber in the original manner.

*Interpretation center:* Sponsored by a modern timber company or educational institution, this could feature indoor and outdoor exhibits depicting the history, science, and technology of forestry and forest products. Action displays could include working models with taped narration.

The entire complex could have an entrance and exit control point that is easily accessible from main transportation nodes. Rather than build drives and parking lots to bring visitors to all of the features, designers

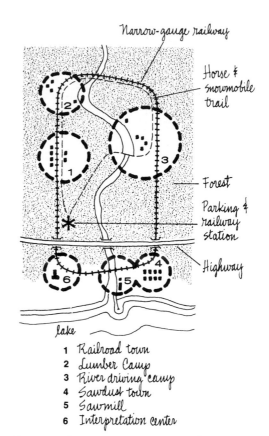

1 Railroad town
2 Lumber Camp
3 River driving camp
4 Sawdust town
5 Sawmill
6 Interpretation center

**5-2.** *Concept for an attraction complex.* Possible elements in a complex designed around the historic theme of lumber production.

could restore a circulating narrow-gauge railway from the turn of the century that would provide access while offering a much more stimulating atmosphere. The redesign of land and building features alike would require skill and creativity together with research results from land analysis.

2. As discussed, a **service community** is an essential element of all destination zones. But this fundamental must be enhanced through better design and planning. When all urban public policies and private developments consider the visitor's needs foremost, destinations will be able to fulfill their functions more efficiently and beautifully. This point is elaborated in the section, "Community Tourism Development."

3. The design of key **circulation corridors** and their accessibility to the community deserve special consideration. These corridors, predominantly highways, are pipelines to such

**5-2.** *Continued.*

services as hotels, eating places, entertainment, and stores for tourists traveling to attraction clusters. Because highways serve such a vital function, their design must go beyond structural engineering and include greater consideration of the traveler's functional needs and visual impressions along the way. Better signage for directions and information is needed. Cooperative agreements and controls are necessary to prevent roadside blight and enhance roadside vistas. Better rest stops require locations near service centers rather than isolated areas where travelers feel less secure. Rest stops must provide more than the bare requirements of today's state-sponsored stops—only toilets and information. Travelers prefer stops that have telephones, snacks, meals, soft drinks, maps, gasoline, and other products and services.

4. **Linkage corridors** tie attraction clusters, the vital organs of destination, to community services. These corridors require design standards different from those that grow out of the traditional engineering emphasis on road design. Much greater sensi-

5-2. *Continued.*

tivity is needed regarding traveler perception, needs, and typical functions. These corridors are entranceways to attractions, and so all roadside views take on great importance in setting the mood for travel objectives. Even roads that pass through ugly strip business or ramshackle neighborhoods can be enhanced greatly through new landscape controls and actions of redesign, regrading, and relandscaping.

Together, the interrelated and interdependent functions of these four main elements make up the destination body. When this concept is implemented, many jurisdictions, designers, developers, and managers will have to bring their individual plans to a common table, and the many stakeholders in destinations will benefit as a result. Of all the design professions, landscape architecture should be taking the most responsibility for implementation.

## TYPES OF ZONES

Study of destination-zone development suggests three types based on spatial relationships.[2] The first, described in figure 5-1, is here called a *radial destination zone*.

Of increasing significance for tourism worldwide is the *urban destination zone* (fig. 5-3). With the recent strides made in urban renewal and historic restoration, and increased trade and improvements in urban amenities, cities have again become major travel targets. However, adapting urban areas to visitor use requires new design approaches. Important tourist elements in cities are attraction complexes, service centers, linkage between service centers and attractions, and linkage with markets.

Again, landscape architects can play a valuable catalytic role in the adaptation of cities to visitor use. Every aspect of adaptation requires special design and management, usually not well understood by public or private urban institutions. It is pertinent to ask how well civic decisions about streets, police, parks, medical services, museums, and maintenance are adapted to visitors.

Urban attractions should be developed with special care. Visitor congestion and conflict with local citizens can be ameliorated by proper design and management. Most visitors arrive by automobile and require special access and parking in order to reach the attractions that interest them. Creative solutions include perimeter parking and shuttle bus access. Downtowns designed to accommodate pedestrians will benefit local citizens as much as visitors.

Urban development for tourists cannot be merely urban cosmetics. After all, those who travel to cities are often friends and relatives of local citizens who take pride in an attractive community with a high quality of life. How the landscape is designed, used, and maintained is critical to local and visitor functions.

A modification of both the urban and radial zones is the *extended destination zone* (fig. 5-4). For many long-distance air travelers, a flight brings them to a major city, but the final

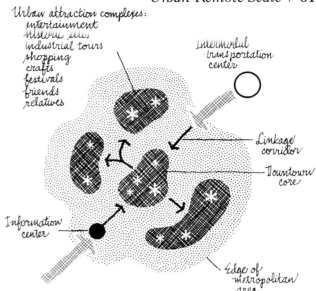

**5-3.** *Urban destination zone.* A city could be analyzed for potential attraction design, development, and management for visitors.

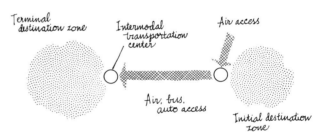

**5-4.** *Extended destination zone.* For long-distance travel, objectives may be reached through stages. Tourists may first travel to a major community and then continue on to a terminal destination zone.

destination, for business or pleasure, is often at a satellite destination zone. Commuter airlines, shuttle buses, or rental cars can provide this linkage. The traveler may or may not utilize the attractions and services of the transfer city.

The design of travel functions within the transfer city must take into account the special needs of those proceeding on to other destinations.

## URBAN-REMOTE SCALE

Figure 5-5 illustrates the destination-zone concept in another way by applying an urban-to-remote scale. For convenience, four zones are suggested. This model brings even remote

# Design for a Purpose

As an aid to the development of tourism, this chapter describes functional relationships for the several attraction classes described in Chapter 4 (table 4-2). These relationships are modeled in several diagrams to show how *access, community, lodging and food service, attraction clusters,* and *linkage* are integrated. Because several classes of attractions are similar in function they may be grouped under a single model. Following is a list of models and attraction classes for touring circuits and longer-stay attraction development (table 6-1). While not exhaustive, these classes and models represent the majority of tourism development patterns today.

## TOURING CIRCUITS

The great diversity of market push and resource pull today stimulates the development of a great variety of places for touring. The following four models diagram the functional relationships for thirteen classes of touring activities. They should be useful in guiding designers toward development that protects resources, enriches visitors' experiences, and stimulates better business.

The diagram in figure 6-1 (Model A) illustrates

functional relationships that are similar for several travel purposes: visiting roadside scenic areas, outstanding natural areas, and touring-circuit camping areas.

This diagram raises several design issues. First is the question of coordinating the design, management, and control of scenic tours. Many firms and agencies produce maps delineating such tours. Others design and manage roads. Yet others control roadside vistas, natural areas, and campsites. Landscape architects could assert leadership in bringing the several actors together for integrated design.

Second is the question of theming. Because of market segmentation each touring circuit requires a dominant theme both in its design and promotion.

A third concern is the length of tours. If a tour is to be created, its length must be in accord with the traveler's time constraints. One solution is to divide long tours into several independent segments.

Fourth, it may be necessary to legislate tour design, at least for some aspects of scenic drives, as has been done in Wisconsin.[1] Zoning laws and other regulations of land use may be the only ways to protect certain unusual scenic values of roadsides. In the American culture, appropriate roadside views for touring include those of such land uses as agriculture, forests, wildlands, and historic sites. Excluded from

Kentucky Dam State Park. (Photo courtesy Tennessee Valley Authority)

designated scenic roads would be waste land-fills, major excavations, heavy industry, signs, billboards, and derelict structures.

Finally, figure 6-2 illustrates a model "hospitality plaza," a concept that could eliminate billboards, a major cause of scenic degradation. By pulling off the highway for information and other travel services, the traveler would no longer be dependent on highway signage. Published guides, maps, directories, and general travel literature would be available. In more heavily traveled areas, trained counselors could offer information about attractions, services, and facilities. Computers could be used more frequently to reduce manpower costs and provide a wealth of guidance to the traveler. Up-to-the-minute information about weather, highway conditions, hours of admission, fees, and capacities of certain attractions could be incorporated into such a system.

The plaza concept could also include a major interpretation function. Indoor and outdoor exhibits could illustrate important points of interest along routes. Models, samples of products, and dioramas might induce the traveler to investigate attractions nearby.

**Table 6-1. Functional diagrams for attraction classes**

**Touring Circuits:**

| | |
|---|---|
| Model A: | Roadside scenic areas |
| | Outstanding natural areas |
| | Touring camping areas |
| Model B: | Water tour places |
| Model C: | Homes of friends, relatives |
| Model D: | Unusual institutions |
| | Shrines, cultural places |
| | Food, entertainment places |
| | Historic buildings, sites |
| | Ethnic areas |
| | Shopping areas |
| | Crafts, lore places |
| | Air tours |

**Longer-stay:**

| | |
|---|---|
| Model E: | Resorts |
| Model F: | Longer-stay camping areas |
| | Hunting/water sports areas |
| Model G: | Organization camping |
| Model H: | Vacation home sites |
| Model I: | Festival, event places |
| Model J: | Convention, meeting places |
| | Gaming centers |
| | Sports arenas |
| | Trade centers |
| | Science, technology centers |
| | Theme parks |
| Model K: | Special case: national parks |

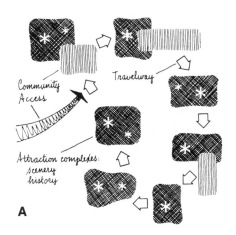

**6-1.** *Model A.* Functional diagram for roadside scenic areas, outstanding natural areas, and touring camping areas.

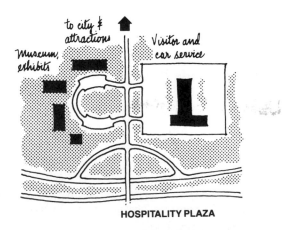

**HOSPITALITY PLAZA**

**6-2.** *Hospitality Plaza.* Good information services at hospitality plazas could eliminate the need for many billboards.

Until billboards were removed, this view from Ala Wai Canal, Hawaii, was blocked. Scenic beauty is a valuable tourism development asset.

In order to serve their true functions, information plazas must be available throughout the nation, not restricted only to state boundaries, as is now the practice of many state governments. In fact, plazas owned by private enterprise and strategically located throughout a country could completely eliminate the need for roadside promotional signage.

## Roadside Scenic Areas

Observing roadside scenery by motor coach or personal car continues to be an important travel interest. But terms such as *shunpike* and *blue highway*—reactions to the deterioration of roadside scenery—suggest real challenges to highway design today.

Where landscape architects have been requested to do so, better highway alignment and better scenic sensitivity have been added to traditional engineering criteria for structural design. It is unfortunate that a national ethic of roadside beauty is so lacking that specially designated scenic highways must be legislated.

## Outstanding Natural Areas

People often take tours primarily to visit especially interesting natural areas along the way to a destination. National, state, and provincial parks and natural reserves contain an abundance of flora and fauna of interest to the travel market.

With regard to natural areas, two design issues are particularly important. First, designers need to analyze the travel corridor from the main route to the natural area for its aesthetic appeal, and to remove anything that detracts from the beauty of the setting. Second, they must address the issue of traveler services. If food, educational, and informational services are needed, they can be designed along the corridor in ways that complement the final tour objective.

## Touring Camping Areas

Camping continues to be an important traveler activity. This market as a whole prefers locations near urban areas rather than special scenic areas. Campers who stop at a place for merely one night require car, food, and, occasionally, motel services, and access to the amenities of nearby cities. Designers should accommodate newer camping trends, such as motor-home travel. Many camp sites, especially those in warm climates, need facilities that serve both touring-circuit travelers and those using the area as a winter destination.

## Water Tour Places

Figure 6-3 (Model B) illustrates an increasingly important travel purpose—water touring. The diagram illustrates functional relationships between the major attraction complex, community service centers, and access.

Today, travelers tour by boat for business as well as pleasure. Conferences and seminars take place on board personal cruisers and huge passenger liners, as well as at urban convention centers. Water travel, no longer a transportation mode but rather a destination complex itself, requires special design consideration.

Ports and harbors, usually located at the "back" sides of cities, need new design treatment to accommodate tourist visits. These entrance points are gateways to exotic cultures and require informational and transitional service centers.

Waterway environments—streams, rivers, canals—offer a unique tourism experience that is growing more popular world-wide. The most outstanding characteristic of inland waterway settings is enclosure. These water courses are always bounded by shorelines, which present a visual edge. As this edge changes with the progress of the boat, so do

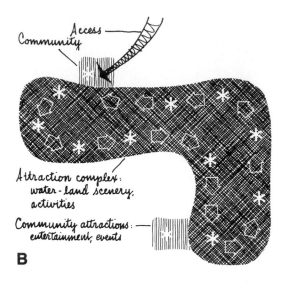

Rise of land or dense plantings can screen other uses — boundaries for a scenic corridor.

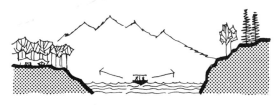

Water-to-land vistas generally upward — produces feelings of protection, enclosure.

6-3. *Model B.* Functional diagrams for water tour places.

the views. Even the smallest land promontory becomes a major curtain, withholding for a moment and then revealing a panorama. Coastal waterway environments usually offer broader vistas than do terrestrial environments.

A variegated land-use pattern along the shore adds interest to a water cruise. But, unfortunately, the sequence is sometimes broken by such intrusions as waste dumps, eroded banks, dilapidated buildings, or, worst of all, outlets pouring forth odorous and toxic wastes.

When these hazards are eliminated, the waterscape offers a unique recreational experience. The water edges of farms, forests, parks, and some cityscapes constitute a separate world of vistas. Objectionable inland land uses can be entirely screened out with only a little landscape development along the edge. The water corridor is an inversion of most highway corridors. Overlooks are turned into "upward-looks" (except along rivers enclosed by levees). Long vistas are over the water, not the land. Furthermore, boat cruising allows much greater maneuverability than does land travel; one can dawdle, stop, or cover great distances in short times.

The key to the design for a water-based environment is the land. The relationship between water and land produces the interest, the tranquility, the drama, the excitement, and the fun of water touring. For example, the reflection of buildings and lights in the night waterscape is magnetic and wholly unique. It can be a spectacular attraction and, indeed, the waterscape is designed more as an attraction than as a travel corridor, although it serves both purposes. A shoreland scenic drive concept is shown in figure 6-4. Suggested is the concentration of major lodging, food, and other services in the community, placing the surrounding resource-based attractions under protective control. By designing special sites for visitor use—beach, overlook, historic site, trail, scenic auto tour—one can offer visitors enrichment and enjoyment without damage to the resources beyond.

In order to avoid conflict, visitor uses of water may need to be allocated on a temporal or spatial basis; some waters are unique for scenic appeals, others for water sports.

## Homes of Friends, Relatives

Visiting friends and relatives is an often-forgotten but dominant travel purpose (fig. 6-5, Model C). This function goes beyond mere contact within residences. Many attractions are visited by travelers because they are en route to or near the homes of friends or relatives. Frequently the visit gives the host the opportunity, and sometimes challenge, of providing a variety of interesting things to see and do. The host residence is used as a base for circuit touring to parks, museums, scenic areas, sports arenas, entertainment, and specialty food services.

Do traffic engineers and city planners consider design linkage for visitors when they establish street systems for residents' homes? Many travelers can testify that no such overt

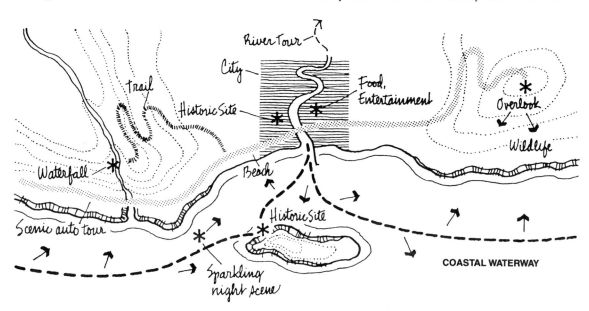

**6-4.** *Coastal waterway.* When designed for both water and land touring, coastal areas can offer special experiences.

## Shopping Areas

For some communities, shopping is the greatest travel objective. Too often, only resident markets are considered when sites are selected for shopping centers. But travelers as well as residents wish to buy clothing, camera film, drugs, camping supplies, and food items. Locations that consider visitor as well as local markets can enhance sales. Feasibility consultants, developers, and designers of shopping complexes should modify their policies to incorporate this innovative approach.

## Craft and Lore Places

Travelers en route to a destination are attracted to sites offering special crafts, paintings, tapestries, carvings, and sculpture, as well as to places that are familiar through legends and lore. The development of such sites, when located near other attractions, adds materially to the pulling power and visitor interest that derive from a larger attraction complex.

## Air Tours

In some regions, the construction of roads or trails would be damaging to the resource base, and sightseeing is best accomplished by helicopter. Well-designed heliports should be associated with other access routes for travelers, as well as with food and lodging services.

One of the greatest advantages of air travel is its geographic scope. Yet this asset is overlooked by all but the most avid landscape buff. Generally, the air traveler has very little help in relating himself to the land he is traversing.

Many travelers on scheduled airlines would probably appreciate a taped narration of the entire flight from take-off to landing. Airlines would not have to produce many tapes, because air routes and travel times vary only slightly from flight to flight, so the project should be economically feasible. The narration could describe cities, farm lands, mountains, and other points of interest along the route. An explanation of the geological formation, historic background, present industrial development, and recreational opportunities of these places might stimulate passengers to visit them on subsequent trips. Maps and descriptive folders, keyed to the narration, could heighten interest.

## LONGER-STAY TRAVEL

In recent years air and expressway travel has enabled tourists to spend longer periods of time at destinations. When people travel long distances they tend to have less interest in attractions en route to a destination than in those at the destination itself, where travel objectives are usually clustered in one general vicinity.

In the following discussion twelve classes of longer-stay travel purposes are illustrated by six functional models. In addition, the special cases of national parks and coastal tourism are described.

## Resorts

Figure 6-7 (Model E) illustrates the general relationship between community, access, attractions, and services for resorts. Conceptually, the modern resort is similar to the organization camp in its relative independence and tight linkage with—almost enclosure by—attraction clusters. Key design considerations are the physical and aesthetic development of attraction clusters, linkage with housing and food service, and linkage with the community. Compatible neighboring uses include other resorts, second-home subdivisions, and extensive-use public parks. Certain resources, such as a warm climate, may encourage the creation of new resort cities. In such cases, designers must encourage the protection of basic attraction resources.

Ranch resorts with cowboy and western themes continue to gain in popularity. These vary along a scale from operating farms and ranches to contrived complexes in ranch-like settings. Farm and ranch businesses maintain their primary functions, perhaps with only slight remodeling of the owner's home to accommodate visitors, but allow merely a few guests at selected seasons. At the other end of the scale are complexes with lodging, food service, country-western entertainment, and other recreational amenities, such as golf courses, tennis courts, pools, and equestrian trails. These require new design input.

Figure 6-8 (Model F) illustrates two classes of development that focuses on natural resources—camping areas and hunting and water sports areas.

## Camping Areas

Adults and families continue to use recreational vehicles at destinations. Older and retired RV users who spend the winter in warm climates usually prefer urban amenities. Park sites often contain central activity rooms, golf courses, hiking trails, and bicycle trails.

Frequently, package tours of these sites expand opportunities for enjoyable and healthful activities. In northern climates, summer use of natural-resource attractions continues to be popular for all age groups. Those who design such places must try to provide an attractive setting for specialized markets that stay at a destination for an extended period of time.

## Hunting and Water Sports Areas

Those who engage in hunting and fishing expeditions may camp near the resource area or occupy a commercial lodging in the nearest community. All facilities close to or within the resource area should be designed to be compatible with the special resource features.

## Organization Camping

For many years young people and adults have engaged in forms of camping exclusive to each group. This purpose is shown in figure 6-9 (Model G). Examples include camps led by the Boy Scouts, Girl Scouts, YWCA, YMCA, and 4-H clubs, as well as by church and conservation groups. In addition to the main goal of

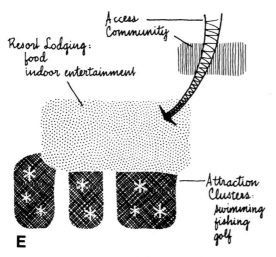

**6-7.** *Model E.* Functional diagram for resorts.

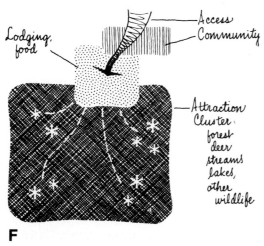

**6-8.** *Model F.* Functional diagram for camping and hunting/fishing areas.

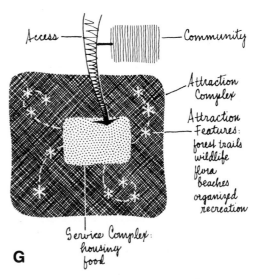

**6-9.** *Model G.* Functional diagram for organization camping.

living close to nature the group may have educational, religious, or fraternal objectives. The development of organization camps is promoted heavily by exponents of outdoor and conservation education, now known as "environmental education."

Although it is a key destination activity, organization camping land use is conceptually the reverse of many others. Attraction clusters surrounding a core of facilities need to be linked by well-designed trails for minibuses, canoe trucks, or other modes of transportation. In order to conserve the natural setting and to increase utility, safety, and control, the planner should concentrate the facilities rather than disperse them.

Compatible neighbors include other organization camps, forests, and other extensive land uses. Second-home subdivisions, public parks and beaches, and service clusters are generally poor neighbors.

## Vacation Home Sites

Figures 6-10 through 6-13 (Model H) illustrate the basic functional relationships appropriate for vacation-home use. Here, the housing development is frequently imbedded in the resource attraction and, often, surrounds it.

Settings and locations vary, but most vacationers seek proximity to water. Some prefer mountains; others wilderness; and a few, urban areas. For all of these users, scenic views, access to water, seclusion, woodland settings, and interesting topography are more important than cost.

Some market segments accept designs that concentrate housing in rows or fourplexes rather than detached units. Often management firms provide such amenities as swimming areas, golf courses, and exercise rooms. Another market segment uses mobile homes stationed at vacation-home sites with similar amenities.

As with all water-oriented uses, designers must respect the limited waterfront. Illustrated in figures 6-11 through 6-13 are three density patterns—all designed to leave the waterfront open. Generally, cars can be kept out of the

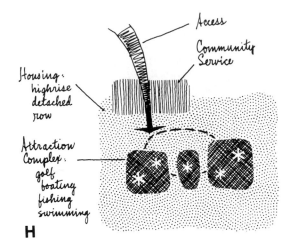

6-10. *Model H.* Functional diagram for vacation home sites.

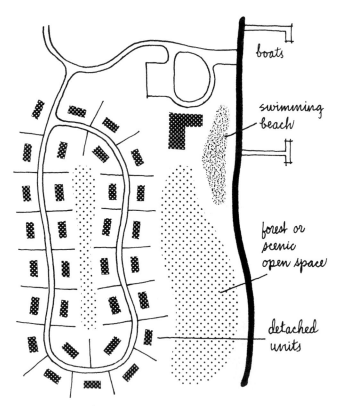

6-11. *Low-density use.*

shore area. Beach views and easy foot access are prime design considerations.

The relationship to community may be very weak or strong depending on the activity patterns desired. Compatible nearby developments are shopping centers, cultural centers,

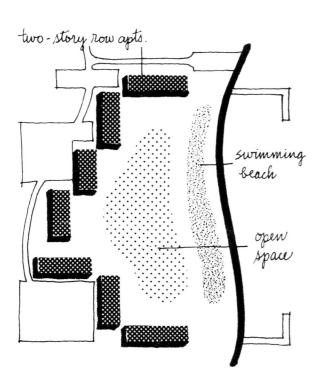

**6-12.** *Medium-density use.*

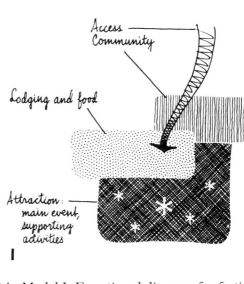

**6-14.** *Model I.* Functional diagram for festival and event places.

and sports complexes. Heavy industry, camps, and intensive-use public parks are not the best neighbors.

## Festival and Event Places

Because they involve only a temporary use of sites, festivals and events are one of the most difficult classes of attractions for designers and developers to create and manage (fig. 6-14 [Model I]). The diagram emphasizes that the event site, lodging and food, and support community are closely related for best function.

While the supporting services and attractions may be permanent, the event thrusts thousands of people into existing streets, parks, and other facilities for only a short time. This places great stress on the capacity and management control of event sites. Considerations of attractiveness, convenience, comfort, safety, and cleanliness are critical. As these attractions grow in popularity, catalytic action will be demanded of the designer to pull together all agencies and organizations involved. Even though transitory, events require policies and decisions that will satisfy the needs of thousands of visitors for short periods of time.

**6-13.** *High-density use.*

could be the foundation for even greater use of national parks and even greater protection of basic resources. This fundamental concept was expressed several years ago in Canada's national-park policy: "The extremes of a zoning plan would be a wilderness area on the one hand and a permanent townsite on the other."[6] A similar concept was set forth in a document of the International Union for Conservation of Nature and Natural Resources: "If parks can be classified into different zones managed to meet different sets of objectives, the tension between perpetuation and use will be minimized."[7] Landscape architect Richard R. Forster's concept includes three zones: a protected resource core limited to scientists only; a partial reserve where visitors are permitted but restricted to authorized trails and parking areas, and an outer zone for recreation and access by tourists. B. K. Downie has suggested a five-zone concept, from special preservation areas to visitor park services.[8]

The following scenario builds on the work of others and suggests a five-zone pattern as shown in the model. It begins with certain basic assumptions:

1. National park boundaries are political, not ecological. The final boundary established is a legislated line that circumscribes an area of varied resources, only some of which are ecologically or culturally significant, rare, or fragile.
2. Within these boundaries the land characteristics are not homogeneous. Some portions may be rare, fragile, or unusual; other portions may have no unusual characteristics and may already show development by man.
3. Policy decrees public use of the land because society can benefit from contact and understanding of the protected resources. Visitors are enriched by exposure to natural and cultural phenomena.
4. An analysis of visitors has shown that, while many can share the experience of key elements of the park, the market tends to segment itself in its use of supportive services (food, lodging, retail sales, entertainment).

5. Some parks attract many more millions of visitors than others because of proximity to population centers, ease of access from markets, or popularity of features.

Certain planning and design concepts could be based on these assumptions. Through land-resource study and analysis of the park and surrounding areas, several zones could be identified. These would provide the designer, developer, and manager with strong foundations for policy. Instead of a blanket policy that erroneously assumes that everything within a park boundary requires the same rules, each of the following zones would have its own set, based on ecological and biological foundations as well as on market considerations.

1. *Key Resource-Protection Zone.* Qualified biologists, landscape architects, historians, and archaeologists could identify the prime resources of the park, including scenic resources, rare plants, important animals and habitats, and areas of architectural, historic, or archaeological value that cannot withstand human intervention. Generally, these will be the features that stimulated the creation of the park in the first place. This zone would be intended only for scientific use.
2. *Wildland/Low-Use Zone.* Within the park, other lands may be less valuable but still contain resources that would be disturbed if roads and facilities were introduced. These areas would constitute a roadless zone with limited human access, much like present areas governed by wilderness policy.
3. *Extensive-Recreation Zone.* Specialists could identify specific areas outside the wildland zone that are extensive and stable enough to support visitor use. Extensive recreation, such as hunting, fishing, and camping, could be provided in accordance with proper planning and design principles. The extent of this development would need to be in balance with the resource base.
4. *Tourist Zone.* Special sites and travelways for motorcoaches, monorails, or other

forms of mass transportation could be installed for visitor use. Proper design of facilities to handle mass use could protect resources and allow public enrichment. For example, travelways could penetrate restricted zones, permitting visitors to see, but not come in contact with, special resources. These travelways would not be open to personal vehicles. Special turnouts, overlooks, and interpretation centers along the way could contain educational exhibits, literature, slide presentations, and lecture rooms.

5. *Service Community Zone.* At the edge of the park, either just inside or outside the boundary, a service community zone could operate independently as a city. All development would flow according to market demand. Today, enough is known about urban design to plan and create attractive, functional, and market-oriented communities. Although new towns may be necessary, it is far better to expand one that has an established infrastructure and management policy.

While it certainly does not address all national park design and management issues, the five-zone concept would resolve many design problems. It would allow millions of visitors to use a park without damaging its resources. The merit of this scenario is demonstrated in several areas where at least some of these principles are practiced.

For example, numbers of red-cockaded woodpeckers, Florida sandhill cranes, round-tailed water rats, and American alligators have actually increased in number at the Okefenokee National Wildlife Refuge. At the same time, the number of visitors has also increased.[9] This is due to the prohibition of personal cars and the use of a rubber-tired interpretive visitor train, which allows visitor enrichment while reducing vandalism in the area and disturbance to wildlife. The concept contributes to what Joseph L. Sax has identified as the four key meanings of national parks: (1) places where recreation reflects the aspirations of a free and independent people; (2) object lessons for a world of limited resources; (3) great laboratories of successful natural communities; and (4) living memorials of human history on the American continent.[10]

When a national, state, or provincial park is zoned in this manner, visitors need to be informed about the zone characteristics and boundaries. Upon entering the park, the visitor could be given a map describing the resources, policies, and functions of each zone. Color coding on the map could correspond to well-designed markers on trails and roads at zone junctures.

Whether this or some other scheme is adopted for national-park planning and design, one principle should be clear: "Most conflict over national park policy does not really turn on whether we ought to have nature reserves (for that is widely agreed), but on the uses that people will make of those places—which is neither a subject of general agreement nor capable of resolution by reference to ecological principles."[11] Design and management should put to rest the polarized dichotomy of resource protection versus public use and strive for the effective operation of both. When designers begin to apply their talents generously and forcefully to this end, they will demonstrate that protection and use can be a happy marriage rather than a cause for divorce.

## SPECIAL CASE: COASTAL TOURISM

Probably no other landform has been as compelling for tourism as the waterfront, especially the coastal zone. This zone is neither land nor water but a special amalgam with more powerful properties than the sum of the two. Places where the land and sea meet not only hold contemporary recreational interest but also evoke nostalgia. "We still like to go beachcombing, returning to primitive act and mood. When all the lands will be filled with people and machines, perhaps the last need and observance of man will be, as it was in the beginning, to come down and experience the sea."[12]

But the linear coast presents special tourism design challenges. For descriptive purposes, it can be divided into four ribbons, each accorded a special use and, thus, special design needs (fig. 6-17).[13]

1. *Neretic*. This ecological "near-shore" zone spreads from the continental shelf to the beach. It is the richest zone for fishing and often contains interesting sandbars and reefs. It is well suited to cruising, sailing, and travel to nearby islands. Visual contact is predominantly with the sea.
2. *Beach*. The beach zone reaches into the water and onto the land. If wide and sandy, it supports the most popular water-based recreation, as well as relaxing, sand-castle-building, beach sports, people-watching, and action and nature photography.
3. *Shoreland*. Behind the beach lies the setting for camping, picnicking, and hiking. The shoreland zone may also support hotels and other service businesses. Visual linkage between land and sea is important.
4. *Vicinage*. The marine coastal backland is the setting for tourist businesses and vacation homes. In this vicinage zone, the coastal scenery is often enhanced by variations in topography and vegetative cover. Nearness and access to the sea are more important than visual linkage.

Historically, the first tourism development along coasts and inland waterfronts was a road parallel and close to the beach (fig. 6-18). This fulfilled the need for access and resulted in building between the road and the beach. In popular beach areas, massive construction walled off access, views, and air circulation from the backlands. Resorts and vacation homes situated behind the new roads faced concrete backsides and garbage containers.

A wiser design would have led to the placement of main service roads farther away from the beach, providing access to all four zones (fig. 6-19). This would have addressed the fact that primary access comes not along the beach but from the inland region, perpendicular to the beach. Such a design would also avoid circulation conflict between pedestrians going from the homes to the beach and automobiles traveling up and down the shoreline. The coastal zone, in spite of its uniform physical characteristics parallel to the water's edge, is not uniform in demand because of coastal communities and primary access to them (fig. 6-20).

For many years designers have proposed the construction of clusters of buildings or high-rise envelopes along coastal zones (fig. 6-21). Had this been done at Miami or Waikiki Beach, much of the present blockage of views and access to the beach could have been avoided. Because this proposal would lead to greater and better use of the waterfront and backland, it is probably more economic.

In the redevelopment of waterfronts, the smells, sounds, and views of remaining port operations are often interesting to visitors. Derelict properties in between these operations could be razed and developed into interesting park spaces (fig. 6-22).

## URBAN WATERFRONTS

Many cities seek ways of rejuvenating downtown areas for visitors and residents. If they have water resources, there is much greater potential for successful redevelopment. Research has shown that development of water resources downtown is influenced greatly by the stability of the water level. This is especially true of urban rivers as is demonstrated by the successful River Walk in the core of San Antonio, Texas. Following an investigation of the potential of many urban waterfronts, a three-phase process for redevelopment was recommended: (1) investigating motivating factors (who is supportive); (2) analyzing site factors (physical assets and limitations); and (3) understanding important external factors (price, regulations, ownership, and access).[14]

As an aid to visualizing waterfront development opportunities, four model sites are illustrated (figs. 6-23 through 6-34). The given diagram for each model represents a typical urban waterfront situation. These were then studied by landscape architects, who created a functional diagram and a concept plan for each of the four hypothetical situations.

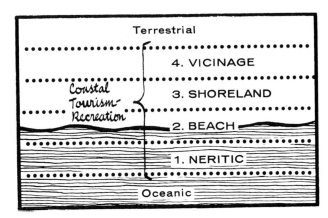

6-17. *Littoral coastal zones.* Four coastal zones with differing tourism design potential.

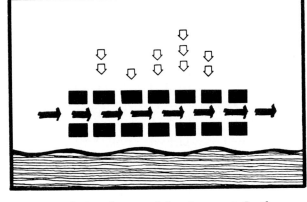

6-18. *Traditional coastal development.* In the past, highways too close to the shoreline have restricted use of this valuable asset to only a few people, blocking views and access from the backlands.

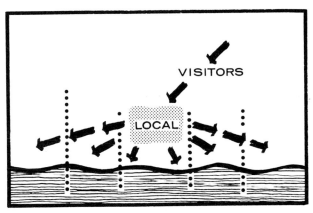

6-19. *Coastal zone protection.* By keeping access highways back and allowing access to segments, one can greatly increase the destination's potential, while protecting the environment.

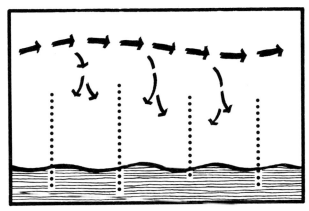

6-20. *Typical approach to coastal attractions.* Residents and visitors most often approach coasts through coastal cities.

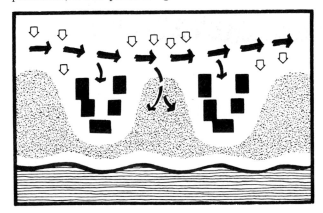

6-21. *Building envelopes.* Groups of structures separated by open space offer an environmentally sensitive solution and protect access and vistas to waterfronts.

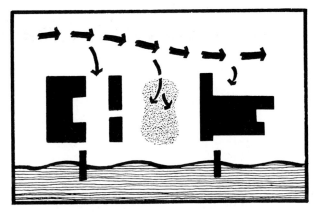

6-22. *Waterfront industrial tourism.* The water's edge holds fascination for visitors, especially if they are given public park access.

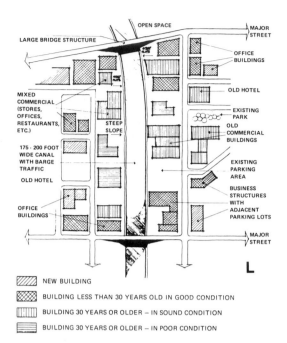

NEW BUILDING

BUILDING LESS THAN 30 YEARS OLD IN GOOD CONDITION

BUILDING 30 YEARS OR OLDER – IN SOUND CONDITION

BUILDING 30 YEARS OR OLDER – IN POOR CONDITION

**6-23.** *Model L.* A typical urban setting in which redevelopment is desired and a canal is built with flood protection.

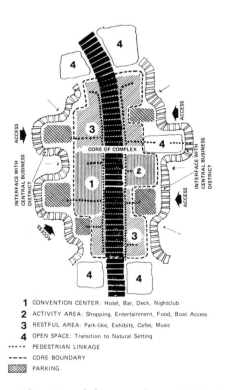

1  CONVENTION CENTER: Hotel, Bar, Deck, Nightclub
2  ACTIVITY AREA: Shopping, Entertainment, Food, Boat Access
3  RESTFUL AREA: Park-like, Exhibits, Cafes, Music
4  OPEN SPACE: Transition to Natural Setting
•••••  PEDESTRIAN LINKAGE
– – –  CORE BOUNDARY
▨  PARKING

**6-24.** A functional diagram for revitalization of waterfront area. The core includes two segments, one straddling the river and the other linking with the business section. A third area could be developed for less active uses.

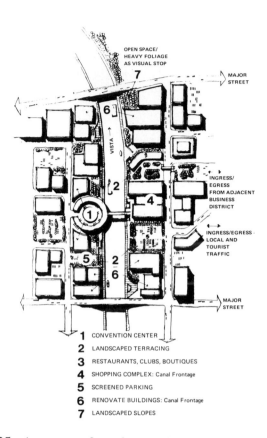

1  CONVENTION CENTER
2  LANDSCAPED TERRACING
3  RESTAURANTS, CLUBS, BOUTIQUES
4  SHOPPING COMPLEX: Canal Frontage
5  SCREENED PARKING
6  RENOVATE BUILDINGS: Canal Frontage
7  LANDSCAPED SLOPES

**6-25.** A concept for solution showing key elements of revitalization for visitor and resident use.

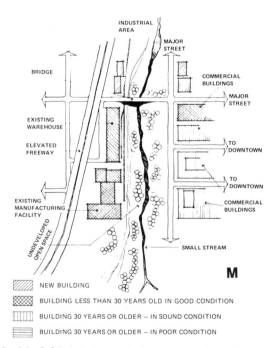

NEW BUILDING

BUILDING LESS THAN 30 YEARS OLD IN GOOD CONDITION

BUILDING 30 YEARS OR OLDER – IN SOUND CONDITION

BUILDING 30 YEARS OR OLDER – IN POOR CONDITION

**6-26.** *Model M.* A typical stream corridor in an industrial urban area.

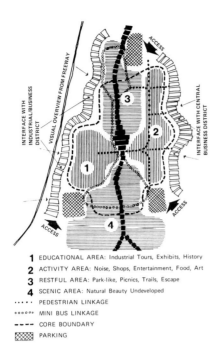

1 EDUCATIONAL AREA: Industrial Tours, Exhibits, History
2 ACTIVITY AREA: Noise, Shops, Entertainment, Food, Art
3 RESTFUL AREA: Park-like, Picnics, Trails, Escape
4 SCENIC AREA: Natural Beauty Undeveloped
····· PEDESTRIAN LINKAGE
∘∘∘∘∘ MINI BUS LINKAGE
---- CORE BOUNDARY
▨ PARKING

**6-27.** A functional diagram for redevelopment, showing activity and restful areas.

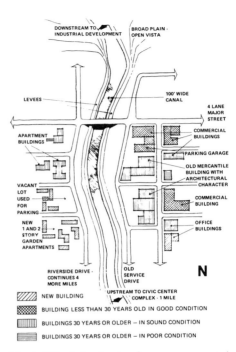

▨ NEW BUILDING
▨ BUILDING LESS THAN 30 YEARS OLD IN GOOD CONDITION
▥ BUILDINGS 30 YEARS OR OLDER – IN SOUND CONDITION
▤ BUILDINGS 30 YEARS OR OLDER – IN POOR CONDITION

**6-29.** *Model* N. A typical urban core containing a navigable river.

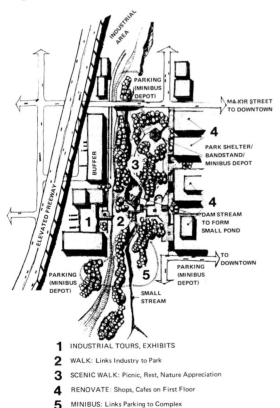

1 INDUSTRIAL TOURS, EXHIBITS
2 WALK: Links Industry to Park
3 SCENIC WALK: Picnic, Rest, Nature Appreciation
4 RENOVATE: Shops, Cafes on First Floor
5 MINIBUS: Links Parking to Complex

**6-28.** A concept for final redevelopment, showing conversion of blighted stream valley to attractive scenic and business uses.

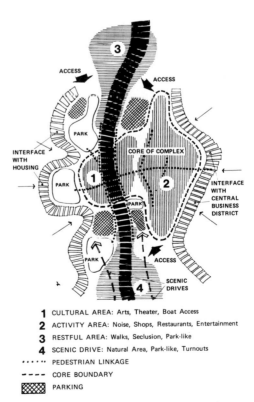

1 CULTURAL AREA: Arts, Theater, Boat Access
2 ACTIVITY AREA: Noise, Shops, Restaurants, Entertainment
3 RESTFUL AREA: Walks, Seclusion, Park-like
4 SCENIC DRIVE: Natural Area, Park-like, Turnouts
····· PEDESTRIAN LINKAGE
---- CORE BOUNDARY
▨ PARKING

**6-30.** Suggested functional elements to be redesigned, including entertainment, convention center, and open space.

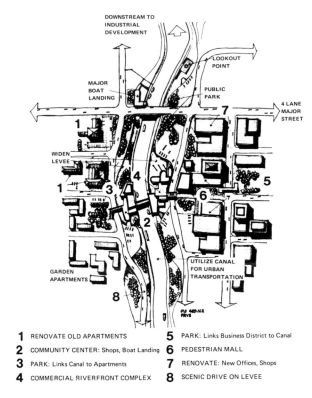

**1** RENOVATE OLD APARTMENTS   **5** PARK: Links Business District to Canal

**2** COMMUNITY CENTER: Shops, Boat Landing   **6** PEDESTRIAN MALL

**3** PARK: Links Canal to Apartments   **7** RENOVATE: New Offices, Shops

**4** COMMERCIAL RIVERFRONT COMPLEX   **8** SCENIC DRIVE ON LEVEE

**6-31.** Conceptual plan for a major visitor center for business and pleasure that makes use of water assets.

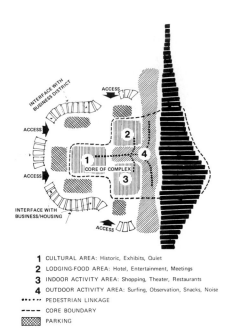

**1** CULTURAL AREA: Historic, Exhibits, Quiet

**2** LODGING-FOOD AREA: Hotel, Entertainment, Meetings

**3** INDOOR ACTIVITY AREA: Shopping, Theater, Restaurants

**4** OUTDOOR ACTIVITY AREA: Surfing, Observation, Snacks, Noise

••••• PEDESTRIAN LINKAGE

– – – CORE BOUNDARY

▨ PARKING

**6-33.** A sketch of proposed functions to make greater use of waterfront and establish better linkage with community.

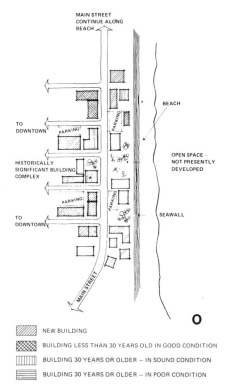

▨ NEW BUILDING

▨ BUILDING LESS THAN 30 YEARS OLD IN GOOD CONDITION

▥ BUILDING 30 YEARS OR OLDER – IN SOUND CONDITION

▤ BUILDING 30 YEARS OR OLDER – IN POOR CONDITION

**6-32.** *Model O.* A typical urban waterfront setting, scheduled for renewal.

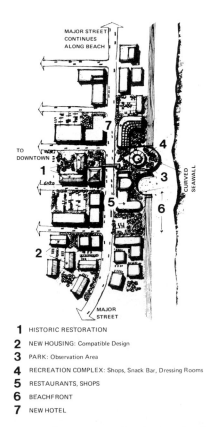

**1** HISTORIC RESTORATION

**2** NEW HOUSING: Compatible Design

**3** PARK: Observation Area

**4** RECREATION COMPLEX: Shops, Snack Bar, Dressing Rooms

**5** RESTAURANTS, SHOPS

**6** BEACHFRONT

**7** NEW HOTEL

**6-34.** A suggested conceptual solution including an overpass to provide pedestrian linkage between the city core and seafront activity.

## SPECIAL POPULATIONS

Greater recognition by society and more abundant legislation concerning the rights and interests of special populations has yielded increasing design responsibility. Especially needed are designs that make travel easier for the mentally ill, mentally retarded, disabled, aged, and sensory impaired, who represent growing travel markets. Although much progress has been made in recent years, barrier-free renovation and new design of tourist-oriented businesses, attractions, and transportation for special populations must be a part of all tourism development.

Design for tourism must be sensitive to the needs of the physically limited. (Photo of the Oregon Dunes Overlook courtesy Terry Slider)

If designers are to properly meet the needs of special travel populations, they should avail themselves of standards and guides for building and site design. For example, *Barrier Free Site Design*, a publication that represents the state-of-the-art for handicap design, provides a multitude of required specifications, recommendations, and examples.

1. Special transportation facilities should be provided for people with restricted use of the exterior environment. Care should be taken to separate various modes of transportation, where practical, since their points of intersection are usually confusing, dangerous, and delaying. Vehicular traffic should be separated as much as possible from bicycle traffic, and both should be distanced from pedestrian traffic.

2. In general, access between transportation facilities and buildings should be smooth and free of barriers that may prove impossible for physically restricted people to negotiate. Paving surfaces should be hard and relatively smooth, curbs should have ramped cuts, walks should be sufficiently wide to accommodate two-way traffic, and entrance walks to buildings should slope gently to the platform before the doors. In buildings where exterior stairs are required, at least one major entrance should be served by a ramp as well.

3. Doors into public buildings should preferably be activated by automatic opening devices. If the cost is prohibitive, horizontal levers or through bars should be installed on the doors.

4. Public conveniences, such as restroom facilities, drinking fountains, telephones, elevators and waiting areas should be well organized and located in close proximity to building entrances. This will allow people with physical limitations to gain access to necessary facilities with a minimal amount of hardship or embarrassment.[15]

Some excerpts from *Barrier Free Site Design* are illustrated in figures 6-35 through 6-38.

# 7/

# Design Principles

Tourism, by its very nature, tends to make all the world the same. There is homogeneity in the chains and franchises proliferated by the business sector. Tourists, while seeking the unique characteristics of different areas, tend to reduce the individuality of place by carrying their cultural baggage with them wherever they go. This is the paradox, and therefore the design challenge, of tourism.

People have abdicated their relationship with land because the modern workplace confines us to an artificial and urbanized environment, denying us the contact with the land that was so vital to our ancestors. Perhaps it is only through travel, especially pleasure travel, that we can recover the fundamental tie between people and place. Upon the designer's shoulders rests the responsiblity of defining the essence of place while satisfying the interests and wishes of continuing flows of outsiders. Landscape architect Garrett Ekbo expressed this concern:

> Will the proprietors and promoters of environments and facilities for tourism, those operators of obsolescent economic and technical structures, those eager opportunists in a modern no-man's land, recognize the possibility for building a program which could be of major aid to modern man in his search for a way out of our contemporary computerized dilemma? . . . Human imagination and creativity have transcended many staggering challenges on the long road from cave to skyscraper. We can hope that they will also conquer this latest and largest problem.[1]

Olympic National Park. (Photo courtesy National Park Service)

Certainly, the answer lies in "imagination and creativity"—the vision of a better use of all resources to offer a more human, a richer, and a more meaningful travel world. "The designer must be able to represent needs and tendencies of the client and the user to himself in order to formulate the design problem. Likewise, he must be able to represent his own intentions to the client in order to develop viable design solutions."[2]

But even when we agree on more creative tourism design as an objective, we seek better directions. Even beyond facts and concepts for better design, can the complicated phenomenon of tourism be given some design structure? Based on the design challenges of tourism described in this book and founded on old and new creative efforts in the reshaping of our land, this chapter contains some guidelines (principles) for stimulating designers to create a better tourism environment.

## BASIC DESIGN

At the outset it should be well understood that all basic design principles established for all design professions apply as well to tourism land use as to any other.[3] Those who create the tourism environment utilize all traditional and contemporary design approaches. A multitude of decisions—for example, those regarding the alignment of drives and walks, the positioning of buildings, and the development of overlooks, as well as the design of building exteriors and interiors—must take into account all the sense perceptions of the user in addition to the many characteristics of basic land resources.

# 8/

# Design Techniques

In recent years the technical side of design has greatly enhanced the entire process from conceptualization through implementation and follow-up. However, as tools, design techniques for tourism are no substitute for inspiration and creativitiy. Rather, they are facilitators.

Of course, manufacturing and construction aids are vital to designers. Improvements in products and equipment have profoundly increased the speed and efficiency of land and building development. Earth can be reshaped, structures can be raised, plants can be transplanted, and land and buildings can be maintained with unprecedented ease. But perhaps the greatest technical changes have been wrought by computers, especially the newer generation of desktop microcomputers. Computer technology is evolving so rapidly that the information in this chapter may be obsolete by the time it is printed. So, the purpose here is not to offer a current catalog, but rather to suggest that all participants—owners, developers, designers, regulators and promoters—maintain close watch over the newer techniques that may be of particular advantage to the tourist.

Four aspects of computers should be em-

phasized. The first, word processing, is so commonplace today that it hardly needs to be mentioned. However, in speeding up and increasing the accuracy of design reporting and record-keeping, word processing has revolutionized office procedures.

A second aspect of computers relates to the market side. Not only are data bases of market segments feasible, but so are market-related graphics. Designers and managers can benefit from software that not only tabulates but also graphically maps current and changing market origins, characteristics, flows, and seasonality.

Computer graphics are perhaps most popular with designers. Many processes once done on the drawing board are now accomplished through computer screens and hard copy. Not only are current situations readily displayed, but alternative scenarios of changes are immediately available for further study.

Another aspect of computer technology needs special emphasis. Computers can be very useful aids in decision making. By readily assessing and manipulating data, they offer reliable information, not merely opinions. Designers, in turn, can provide this information to public groups more quickly, clearly, and convincingly, without long, confusing, and even boring meetings.

Following is a potpourri of techniques that, even though they overlap and are far from complete, may stimulate the interest of the un-

---

Navajo National Monument. (Photo: Fred Mang, Jr., courtesy National Park Service)

initiated. The fear of computer technology is probably the greatest cause of nonuse. The items described here are gleanings from several sources and have many different objectives. Readers are encouraged to engage in open dialogue about how new techniques can improve the task of developing better designs for tourism environments.

## COMPUTER AS DESIGN MEDIUM

Charles M. Eastman has identified five design representation functions of which computers are now capable:

1. *Spatial modeling.* Today's computers not only represent stick figures but can also show enclosed shapes, faces, edges, and vertices. These can be moved, enlarged, reduced, assembled into new forms, and copied.
2. *Representation of performance and functional relations.* Attributes can be assigned to these entities: cost, heat loss, structural strength, and interaction of these factors. Cost estimation and measurements of efficiency of systems can be made.
3. *Database management of logical relations.* Computers can provide immediate checking between components—correct unknowing mistakes, consistency between drawings, and congruency with specifications.
4. *Design development.* The computer is a natural device for abstraction; it can readily reorganize and present information, especially to explore several design possibilities.
5. *Design coordination.* Of particular importance in tourism applications is the extent to which computer use can be an effective means of coordinating the many design disciplines on a large project. It can aid in communication between designers; can be "frozen" so that alternatives can be approved by all involved.[1]

Meir Gross summarizes new computer applications to landscape architecture as a blending of traditional intuitive and perceptual

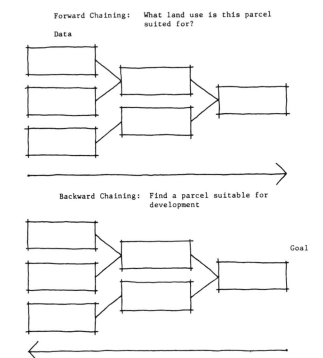

8-1. *Forward and backward chaining.* The data-driven control strategy begins with the data (available in the database) and selects and applies rules that match the current situation. In contrast, the goal-driven control strategy begins with predetermined goal (specified by the user) and selects and applies rules that will achieve that goal.

design with scientific knowledge and quantitative assessment procedures, for which computers are a remarkable aid.[2] It is not a matter of replacing something old with something new but of increasing the speed, accuracy, and ease of communication with which designs can be prepared and presented.

Figure 8-1 illustrates the capability of computers to handle both forward and backward chaining.[3]

## COMPUTER GRAPHICS

One of the most effective tools of the landscape architect is the ability, through training and experience in perspective drawing, to make view sketches of a proposed design. Renderings of buildings and landscapes are basic means of communicating with clients.

William Johnson, who has effectively used sketch techniques, throughout years of successful design work, is now turning to computer-aided graphics. "Graphic communication opens the door of the mind so that people can view and participate in the design process. . . . The product is more fitting; it is more creative and fresh; new ideas are generated."[4]

Johnson begins with rapid and dynamic sketch expressions of concepts that are functional and not too detailed. If too much precision is offered at the start, important policy and functional relationships may be missed. Then he uses the computer to bring up existing perspectives that can be modified as needed.

For example, a ski resort community in the Colorado Rockies was planned for an environmentally sensitive valley. Both physical impact and visual change were of concern. Instead of using costly and time-consuming scale models, Johnson created "before and after" views of development.

In order to establish ground truth, balloons were raised on lines to given heights and to mark boundaries of proposed building sites. When photographed from a helicoper, the resulting information was used to sketch proposals. By using three-dimensional computer simulation, Johnson created views of existing and proposed situations much more rapidly than he would have through traditional sketching techniques.

## DESIGN-RESOURCE COMPARISON

The microcomputer was used effectively by one firm to compare a concept for development of 8,744 acres with resource characteristics to determine degree of environmental compatibility.[5] The purpose was to find out the extent of adverse impact on the natural environment with particular reference to a nearby river.

Using the ERDAS 400 system, designers digitized several key resource characteristics on computer maps, stored them in a polygon format, and analyzed them in a grid-cell format. The resource characteristics were flood plain and drainage areas, erosion/sedimentation potential, slope and soil stability, and vegetation and wildlife.

The results showed that the designer's plans took into account the environmental conditions and avoided development of areas with potential negative impact:

- Less than 1% of the developer's property designated as the least suitable for development was planned for development.
- Less than 1% of the developer's property possessing high potential for erosion/sedimentation was planned for development.
- The majoritty of the development plan was designated for areas that possessed compatible or lower-sensitivity conditions.

## VISUAL SIMULATION

The U. S. Bureau of Land Management has engaged several technicians to pool their talents for the publication *Visual Simulation Techniques*.[6] In it are described:

**Manual Techniques**
Freehand drawing
Rendering from a projected slide
Diazo print
Rendering on a photograph
Etching on a slide
Multi-image printing
Photomontage
Scale model

**Projection Techniques**
Single overhead
Slide/overhead
Overslide (overhead)
Slide-projected montage
Multiscreen
Multi-overhead

**Computer Techniques**
Computer perspective montage
Desktop computer perspective plots

These techniques vary greatly in time and cost but all are effective for simulated illustration. Such graphics aid both the designer and client in visualizing planned development and are especially well adapted to tourism projects, because surrounding environmental settings are always important.

## PERSPECTIVE PLOT

Because the USDA Forest Service is mandated to consider the visual impact of timber harvest patterns, it has developed a program called PERSPECTIVE PLOT.[7] This program accurately and quickly produces three-dimensional plots from one or a series of specific viewpoints. Because it has applications to many other land-form changes, it should be of interest to designers and planners of environmental changes for tourism.

Figure 8-2 illustrates a simulated landscape modification using the PERSPECTIVE PLOT program. This shows proposed ski run development of the Beaver Creek Ski Area in central Colorado. This was done as part of the visual assessment work by the USDA Forest Service. Such drawings have been useful not only to the designers of proposed projects but also to public groups that may be impacted by changed environments. These graphics have assisted communication and decision making among all prime actors and have also been used by landscape architects to simulate effects of road building and dam construction.

In order to improve on the limitations of PERSPECTIVE PLOT, the USDA Forest Service has created a NEWPERSPECTIVES program.[8] This is more user-friendly and better adapted to more computer systems. This software works from a base terrain, coordinated data, vegetative descriptive data, and graphical primitives to produce true-perspective depictions of these features, singularly or in combination, on a CRT or a multipen line plotter.

Another advance in the creation and display of graphic information is PLOT7, developed on the Willamette National Forest (fig. 8-3). This program eliminates much of the hand modification required with earlier methods. PLOT7 automates the display of geographic information in Grid Mapping Systems, producing full color or black-and-white maps at a

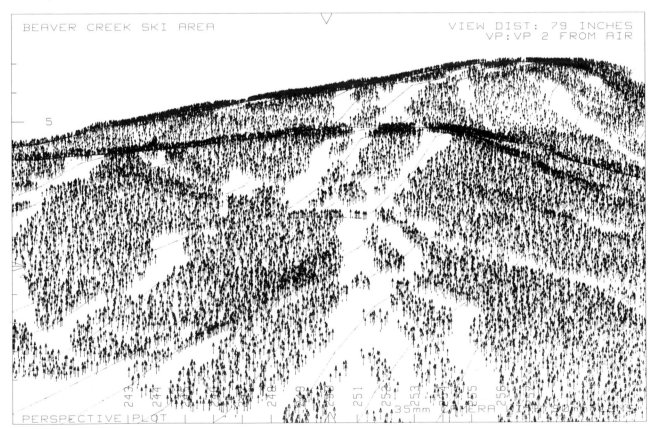

**8-2.** *Computer sketch of ski runs.* View of a mountain slope prepared with PERSPECTIVE PLOT shows how proposed ski runs for the Beaver Creek Ski Area would appear.

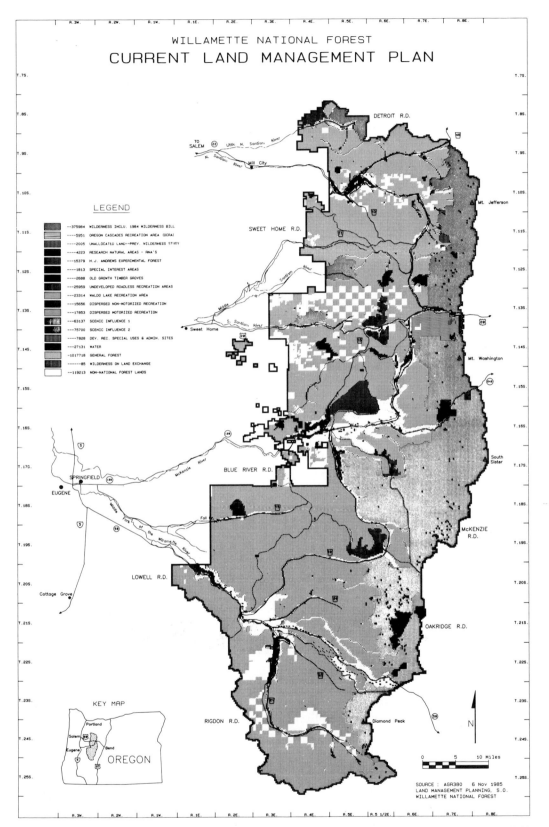

**8-3.** *Willamette National Forest zones.* This current land-management plan, showing many different land uses, was prepared through the use of PLOT7.

manageable scale and quality not possible with hand methods.

Shown here is a land-management map of the Willamette National Forest, including bodies of water, recreational areas, timber groups, undeveloped land, wilderness, and a number of other categories important for future environmental planning.

PLOT7 has proved to meet the need for greater internal communication among staff during study and planning and also between the USDA Forest Service and the several public groups involved. Incidental to the development of these maps has been the finding of new patterns and relationships of land development not apparent before, especially when printed in color.

## LANDSAT

LANDSAT can assist the landscape architect in land-analysis projects related to the development of tourism. Because it is obtained in digital form, it is more compatible with computer mapping than with traditional base maps and airphotos. LANDSAT can provide quantities of land-cover information at far less cost than traditional methods. The rise in the use of microcomputers and increased costs of labor suggest greater use of LANDSAT for tourism planning in the future.

An example of the capability of LANDSAT for land-use analysis is that produced by the Minnesota Land Management Information System (MLMIS).[9] Figure 8-4 shows a black-and-white printout of eight land types for an area near White Bear Lake.

The analysis was performed in three steps. First, the LANDSAT was converted to grids on the MLMIS. Then, data were classified using several techniques. Finally, data were checked with ground data obtained from field checks, which Minnesota has found to be a relatively inexpensive data source. Technicians remind users, however, that LANDSAT records reflectance of land features, not land use. It would appear that LANDSAT is adaptable to recreational and tourism analyses, especially on a regional scale.

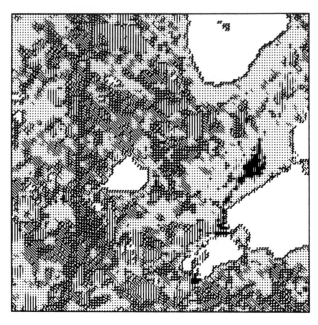

SYMBOL   LEGEND

```
::   1  FORESTED
II   2  CULTIVATED
     3  WATER
#    4  MARSH
#    5  URBAN RESIDENTIAL
%    7  PASTURE AND OPEN
■    8  URBAN NON-RESIDENTIAL OR MIXED
        RESIDENTIAL DEVELOPMENT
```

8-4. *Land types from Landsat.* A composite map prepared with MLMIS shows eight land types for the area near White Bear Lake, Minnesota.

The need for shared computational resources and data archives has stimulated the development of such remote sensing systems as the Digital Image Analysis Laboratory (DIAL) at the University of Massachusetts.[10] DIAL is tailored specifically to analyze LANDSAT and it provides capabilities for projects of almost any size. The growing interest in LANDSAT has stimulated many vendors of "value-added" products and services.

## VIDEOTAPE

Some technicians use videotape and computer images to improve the visual communication of designs. The public's familiarity with television presentations and the utility of the video format make video appealing for large audiences who view presentations through cable networks:

Beyond producing good quality, realistic simulations, the format offers extensive possibilities: simply video-taping the output images and incorporating them into site analysis video footage will be a powerful tool. "Slide-show" programs can display images from the microcomputer memory, dissolving from one image to the next in various dramatic ways. Complete images can be transmitted by modem or telephone line to remote sites almost instantaneously.[11]

Architects are employing video manipulation systems as a design aid within the office and a means of communicating concepts to clients. The basic components of these systems, now available even for small offices, include:

Computer System
    Microprocessor (640K RAM)
    Monitors (color display)
    Painting device (digitizing tablet and stylus)
    Software (for manipulation)

Video Hardware
    Video camera
    Video cassette recorder
    Video editor

Generally, three steps are required for the development of video presentations by computer: the storyboard and script phases (preproduction), image generation (production), and the video editing phase (postproduction). An application of the process is described below.

1. *Preproduction.* The designer checked sketch plans against the actual site by laying video images of a scale model over captured images of site context. These massing studies enabled him to establish building height and mass relationships. Next he wrote a script that included three parts: first, a computer-simulated aerial flight around the proposed building; second, a sequence of views obtained by a person walking up the entrance to the building; and third, views of the site with and without the building.

2. *Production.* In this most time-consuming phase, the designer videotaped the site context, constructed scale models, videotaped the models, and generated computer graphics. The decision to make scale models rather than perspective drawings or computer-generated perspectives was based on office capability. The raw footage of videotape provided the base from which a final tape could be produced. Computer manipulation and print devices were used to generate graphics for title, site context, and building orientation.

3. *Postproduction.* In this final stage, raw footage of videotape was reviewed against the storyboard topics and desirable time sequence. "Off line" editing was done on equipment other than that used for video editing. This produced a series of slides, which were then linked to create a continuous video flow. "On-line" editing produced the final videotape.[12]

## GEOGRAPHIC INFORMATION

Micro-GIS (μ-GIS) is a microcomputer-based geographic information system that can perform many of the operations previously unique to larger computers. This vector-based system features input, storage, analysis, retrieval, and portrayal of spatial data in vector format. Data overlays or intersections are performed, providing theme maps as screen images or hard-copy output. Figure 8-5 provides a system overview of μ-GIS.[13]

Spatial data are captured by using free-cursor digitizer input with immediate display to

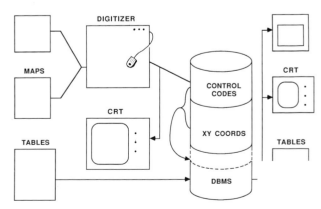

**8-5.** *System overview of μ-GIS.* Basic steps in the process of the geographic information system, with data input and final output of maps, CRT, or tables.

the color monitor. A summary description of system input is as follows:

- All data are captured as points, lines, or polygons.
- Polygons are entered as arc segments, with arcs labeled to identify polygons that share a common line segment.
- Registration of multiple data layers to a single basemap is performed with the use of control pointers.
- Multipurpose line formatting allows linear features to serve multiple functions (for example, road and polygon boundaries).
- Editing features include line deletion and line, point, and polygon numbering.
- Maps at variable scales may be entered as layers to a common basemap.
- Feature-type labeling for linear and point data provides codes for line type on video screen or hard-copy plot.
- Spatial pattern routines estimate areas for polygons and lengths for linear networks.
- Perimeter distance is estimated for all polygons.
- Exterior polygons are separated and compensated for nested interior polygons.
- Point, linear, and polygonal data may be entered in a single file or as separate data layers registered to the basemap.
- Error trapping prevents incorrect feature labeling.

All spatial data are stored on fixed or floppy disks and are referenced by file name. Attributes for associated spatial features are entered into the GIS via the Knowledge Man DBMS. Spatial data files are linked to the DBMS by file name. Searches of the attribute data files are performed utilizing a list of the variables stored in the DBMS.

The μ-GIS program was developed as a stand-alone microcomputer-based GIS that could fulfill the needs of resource managers whose land holdings were small enough (or sufficiently subdivided) to use the microcomputer framework. The number and complexity of the maps, as well as the number and length of stored variables, determines the applicability and speed of μ-GIS's operation. While the process for accomplishing these techniques is not yet as simple as it might be, it is opening up an entirely new world of potential for the designer, certainly for tourism environments.

The National Park Service now uses μ-GIS environmental analysis, not only for new parks but for better management of existing parks (fig. 8-6).[14] Its purpose is to show landscapes that are visible from diverse vantage points; determine areas, distances, and lengths; integrate themes to produce a composite; develop new maps and analyses; and detect changes, analyze trends, or project future possible conditions. The U.S. Fish and Wildlife Service has developed a similar system, called SAGIS.

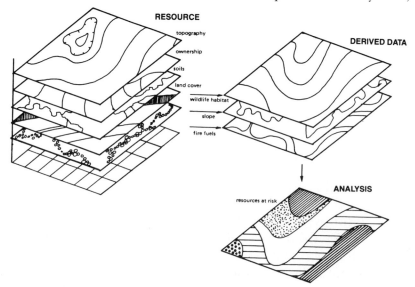

8-6. *GIS of National Park Service.* A diagram of the dominant geographic information system application within the National Park Service.

# REGIONAL ASSESSMENT
# OF POTENTIAL

The computer is a very useful tool for helping designers identify potential tourism destination zones.[15] Because it can readily and inexpensively aggregate map overlays, it is far more efficient and yields better results than the tedious hand-tracing process of the past.

The assessment method described here is based on several assumptions: that certain physical factors are important for destination development; that the greater the abundance and quality of these factors, the greater their potential; and that where more of these factors occur, tourism potential is greatest.

This method requires the following steps:

1. Mapping physical factors
2. Assigning weights to factors
3. Computer mapping of all factors
4. Aggregating all factors
5. Concepts for development

Based on research and observation of areas successfully developed for tourism, the following nine categories of factors have been determined:

| | |
|---|---|
| Water, waterlife | Existing attractions, |
| Topography, | industries, |
| soils, geology | institutions |
| Vegetative cover, | History, ethnicity, |
| wildlife, pests | legends |
| Climate, | Service centers |
| atmosphere | Transportation, |
| Aesthetics | access |

These categories are based on a dependency hierarchy: market interests and activities take place in establishments, which depend on the development of destinations, which in turn depend on factors favorable for development that meets market needs.

This assessment method is a *prefeasibility* process and excludes other final-phase factors important to development, such as finance, labor, management, land availability, cost, and zoning. These final-phase factors can be applied after one identifies areas with greatest

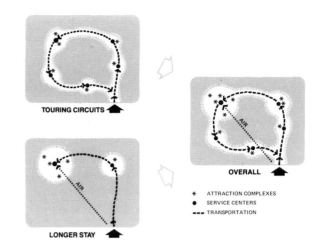

**8-7.** *Regional analysis.* Diagram illustrates concept of finding potential destination zones for touring circuits and longer-stay. When combined, these maps identify areas of overall potential.

potential. Figure 8-7 illustrates how destination zones can be determined for touring circuits and longer-stay tourism and combined for overall potential. Figures 8-8 through 8-12 show how the assessment method was applied to a region of Texas.

*Step 1. Mapping physical factors.* Based on secondary data, outline maps are drawn to a convenient and common scale for the selected region. These outline the general zone locations of each of the nine categories of factors. For each category, narratives are prepared to document characteristics and distribution important to development. This step reinforces map delineation and supports further steps.

*Step 2. Assigning weights to factors.* Because all factors are not of equal importance for tourism, a panel of developers, planners, and designers can be employed to assign relative weights both for *touring circuits* and *longer-stay development.* Table 8-1 illustrates the result of weighting the several factors used in this example. In this case, the panel assigned over three times as many points to transportation than to water for touring-circuit potential, whereas water was assigned about the same as transportation for longer-stay development.

*Step 3. Computer mapping of factors.* Several microcomputer programs are now available that digitize factor maps. Some can manipulate data and create maps that simulate changing conditions, for example, proposed highways, reservoirs, or parks.

*Step 4. Aggregating factors.* By aggregating all factors, one can prepare a composite map that reveals areas where the combination of factors supports or discourages new tourism development (see figs. 8-9 and 8-10).

*Step 5. Concepts for development.* Composite maps, together with descriptive narratives prepared in step 1, provide information about the developmental potential of a region. Planners and designers can then create concepts for touring-circuit and longer-stay destinations (see figs. 8-11 and 8-12). Governments, nonprofit organizations, or commercial enterprises can review these maps and descriptions as a basis for further investigation of the feasibility of specific sites and projects.

After identifying areas with tourism potential, planners can examine the destinations for possible environmental stress. Important natural and cultural resources are likely to be at the core of potential destinations. Knowing this, planners can recommend zoning hierarchies that would protect unusually rare or fragile resources while enabling the development of locations for visitor use.

**Table 8-1. Weighting of tourism development factors**

|  | Touring Circuits | Longer-stay |
|---|---|---|
| Water, water life | 8 | 24 |
| Topography, soils, geology | 10 | 10 |
| Vegetative cover, wildlife, pests | 7 | 8 |
| Climate, atmosphere | 3 | 13 |
| Aesthetics | 13 | 7 |
| Existing attractions, institutions | 10 | 5 |
| History, ethnicity | 9 | 3 |
| Service centers | 15 | 10 |
| Transportation, access | 25 | 20 |
|  | 100 | 100 |

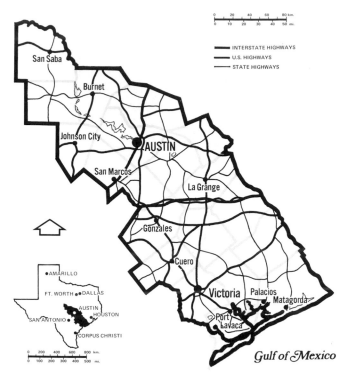

8-8. *Study location.* Map of a twenty-county portion of Texas where potential was evaluated through a regional analysis.

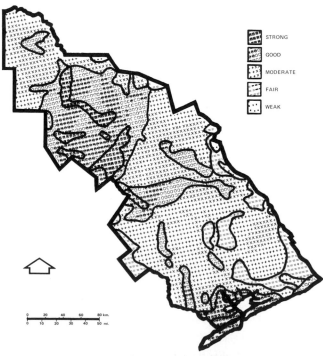

8-9. *Analysis: touring circuits.* Computer map of composite of nine factors for touring-circuit tourism potential. Darker areas show highest potential.

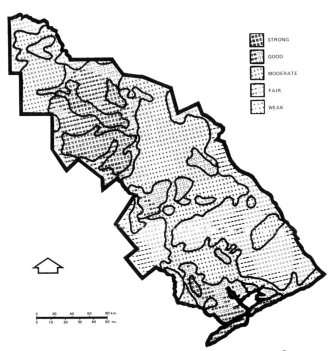

STRONG
GOOD
MODERATE
FAIR
WEAK

0  20  40  60  80 km.
0  10  20  30  40  50 mi.

**8-10.** *Analysis: longer-stay.* Computer map of composite of nine evaluation factors for longer-stay tourism potential. Darker areas show highest potential.

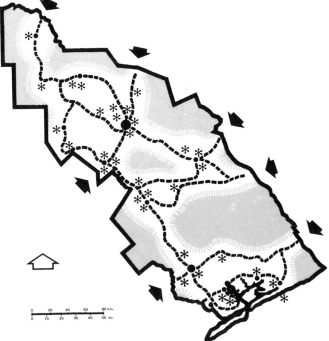

0  20  40  60  80 km.
0  10  20  30  40  50 mi.

**8-11.** *Concept: touring circuits.* A concept diagram of potential touring circuits. Stars are general locations where resource analysis indicates potential for new attraction complexes. Arrows indicate points of entrance from markets.

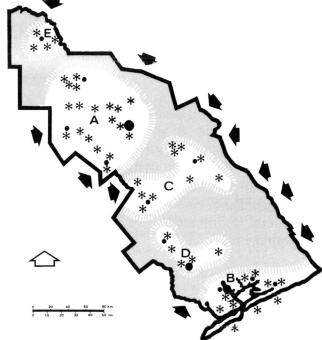

0  20  40  60  80 km.
0  10  20  30  40  50 mi.

**8-12.** *Concept: longer-stay.* A concept diagram of potential longer-stay destination zones. Research revealed potential for five zones. Stars are general locations where analysis indicates potential for attraction complexes.

# 9/
# Gallery of
# Well-Designed Places

This gallery of travel-oriented design is a sampling of works well done. It proves that many of the issues and problems described in the earlier chapters of this book can be solved. Many contemporary designers, like landscape architect Edward D. Stone, Jr., testify that, today, corporate clients, particularly proprietors of hotels and resorts, are more willing to listen to the advice of an experienced landscape architect. In a recent review of hotel and resort design, including Stone's work, one writer characterized landscape architects as "those complex hybrids of artist, craftsman, psychologist, sociologist, and down-to-earth, bottom line wizards."[1]

The following cases present a random cross section of award-winning, outstanding, unusual, and successful designs by landscape architects, architects, and others. The success of the designers is measured by their mastery of all three types of function—structural, physical, and aesthetic. While space does not permit

Oregon Dunes Overlook. (Photo courtesy Terry Slider)

a complete survey of tourism development, these examples include attractions and services that have varied requirements, a broad geographic range, and typical and atypical problems. Designers and developers can learn much from these solutions and use that knowledge to create future landscapes and structures for tourism.

These brief descriptions and illustrations imply more than they reveal. They imply a new breadth of design professionalism than is popularly understood. Modern decision makers in tourism, from the smallest entrepreneur to the largest corporate owner or governmental agency, must follow a series of important steps leading from the first idea to opening day. And even then, the process continues, for designs must also be evaluated *after* they are implemented. As professional designers become more knowledgeable about the functions of tourism, they will provide a coordinating and integrating role along every step of the way. Each example illustrates this fusion of creative ideas and practical decisions from inception to realization.

# Point State Park, Pittsburgh, Pennsylvania

*GWSM, Landscape Architects*

A generous open space in the heart of an industrial city, Point State Park provides dramatic vistas as well as repose. The design is large in scale, yet marries expressway travel to pedestrians and offers memorable views of the confluence of the historic Monongahela and Allegheny rivers. The well-placed fountain, in scale with the entire setting, provides an accent in motion.

Broad river valley park and fountain accent. (Photo courtesy GWSM, Inc.)

Cantilevered overlook at Point State Park offers access to dramatic views. (Photo courtesy GWSM, Inc.)

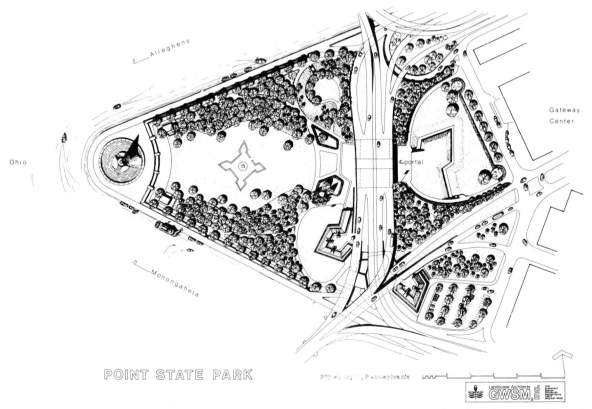

Plan of Point State Park showing design compatibility between expressway and pedestrian use. (Drawing courtesy GWSM, Inc.)

# Tom McCall Waterfront Park, Portland, Oregon

*Mitchell Nelson Group, Inc., Landscape*
*Architects*

This solution superbly meets the challenge of designing a multipurpose park in a rundown urban core. As an award jury commented, this area is now "a spacious, sufficiently formal, park-like area, uncluttered by constructions and ingenious walls, fountains, steps, etc. Serves everyday leisure activities and certainly increases the dignity of the city."[2] Visitors and residents can now enjoy repose, exciting festivals, or boat access in the very heart of the city.

Open entertainment near water's edge. (Photo: James Lemkin)

Waterfront beauty and boat access in the heart of a large city. (Photo: James Lemkin)

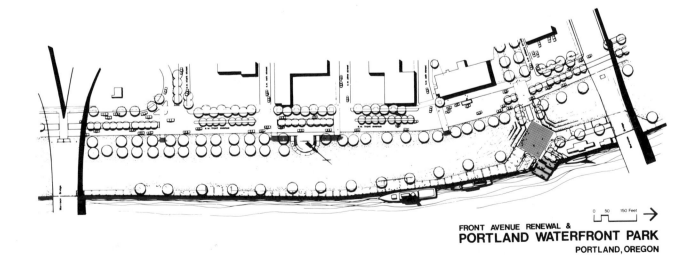

FRONT AVENUE RENEWAL &
**PORTLAND WATERFRONT PARK**
PORTLAND, OREGON

Plan of Portland Waterfront Park showing park and boat access (*at right*).

# Lakes Park, Lake County, Florida

*Sasaki Associates, Inc., Landscape Architects*

The main design challenge of this 279-acre park was converting an abandoned rock quarry into a popular recreational place for vacationers and residents. Located just south of Fort Meyers, the park now features a white sand beach (added silica sand two-feet thick for 900 feet), a marina, picnic shelters, nature trails, boardwalks, a fitness course, an amphitheater, and a café. The beach area is enclosed by an anchored vinyl fabric curtain, where 1 million gallons of water are circulated daily for stable water quality. Many unusual soil conditions of the site required special engineering and plant modifications.

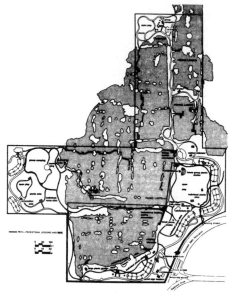

Plan of Lakes Park showing many islands and ribbons of land in an old rock quarry. Dark line indicates a jogging and bike trail. (Drawing courtesy Sasaki Associates, Inc.)

View of developed sand beach along the edge of an old quarry. (Photo courtesy Sasaki Associates, Inc.)

Excellent design of public access and environmental protection. (Photo courtesy Sasaki Associates, Inc.)

# South Dunes Interpretive Walk and Beach, Jekyll Island, Georgia

*Robinson Fisher Associates, Landscape Architects*

Once a millionaire's playground, this island is now managed by Georgia's Jekyll Island Authority. Following a new land-use policy for the entire island, which had eroded badly, the designer's objectives for the beach area were to restore the stability of the dunes; recreate the freshwater slough; and re-educate the public about the nature and value of the island's environment. Since redesign, the dunes are stabilizing, people enjoy greater access to the beach, and the natural beauty and ecology of the area have been restored.

General plan showing relationship between restored dune area, redeveloped slough, and interior of South Dunes park. (Drawing courtesy Robinson Fisher Associates)

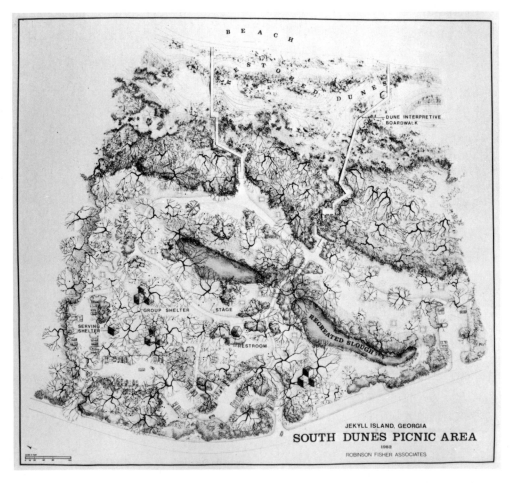

JEKYLL ISLAND, GEORGIA
SOUTH DUNES PICNIC AREA
1982
ROBINSON FISHER ASSOCIATES

Group shelter area on less sensitive resource portion of newly designed park. (Photo courtesy Robinson Fisher Associates)

Design of boardwalk solves dune erosion problem and provides for an interpretive adventure. (Photo courtesy Robinson Fisher Associates)

Overall view of beach and dune area of park. (Photo courtesy Robinson Fisher Associates)

# Oregon Dunes Overlook, Florence-Reedsport, Oregon

*Terry Slider and Bond & Associates,
Landscape Architects*

To solve visitors' increasing demands for access to natural resources, the Oregon Dunes Overlook, a prime example of integrated design, provides viewing decks, boardwalks, picnic sites, interpretive signage, and rest rooms. According to an award jury, it is "an imaginative way of accessing a very precious ecosystem, dramatic public approach, [and] a major public education statement in an exciting direction by the Forest Service."[3]

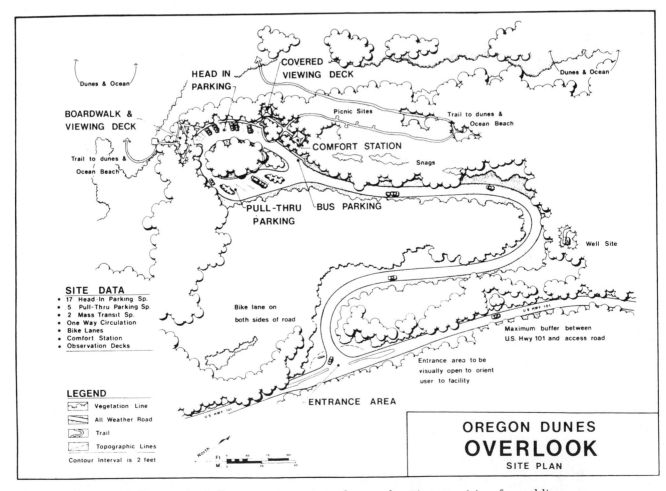

Plan of Oregon Dunes Overlook illustrates retention of natural setting provision for public access.
(Drawing courtesy Terry Slider)

Stairs prevent erosion caused by walking over dunes. (Photo courtesy Terry Slider)

Overlook provides for visitor interest as well as resource protection. (Photo courtesy Terry Slider)

# Westonbirt Visitor Centre, Gloucestershire, England

*Andris Berzins & Associates, Architects*

Adapting to greater volumes of tourists, designers are creating functional and attractive visitor centers appropriate to each setting. This structure-and-landscape complex, a focal point for the entire arboretum, is an organic design solution for a dominantly vegetative setting. The main pavilion contains flexible exhibition space, a seminar/audiovisual room, a library, and offices for staff. The adjacent pavilion forms a courtyard, provides refreshments, and is rotated 45 degrees to the main pavilion to create design tension between the two forms. The structures relate superbly to the site, a 150-year-old arboretum containing two thousand trees of fifty-five species.

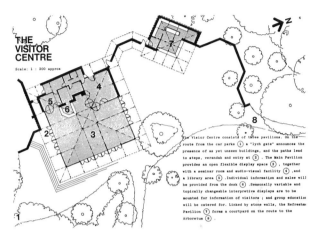

Plan showing environmental orientation of Westonbirt Visitor Centre structures. (Drawing courtesy Forestry Commission)

Visitor center design provides necessary functions and yet blends well with the setting. (Photo courtesy Forestry Commission)

# Miner's Castle Overlook, Munising, Michigan

*Johnson, Johnson & Roy/inc., Landscape Architects*

This redesign of a heavily impacted resource accommodates large numbers of visitors while arresting the heavy erosion of the land that had occurred in the past. Miner's Castle Overlook is only one part of an attraction complex, the Pictured Rocks National Lakeshore, owned by the National Park Service. Several new overlooks, a comfort station, new trails, a relocated entry drive, and facilities adapted to the handicapped are part of the overall design, which mitigates visitor impact to retain landscape quality.

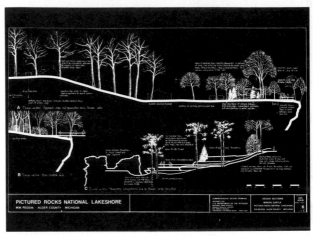

Studies of improved design of walks, overlooks, and relocation of camping. (Drawing courtesy Johnson, Johnson, & Roy/inc.)

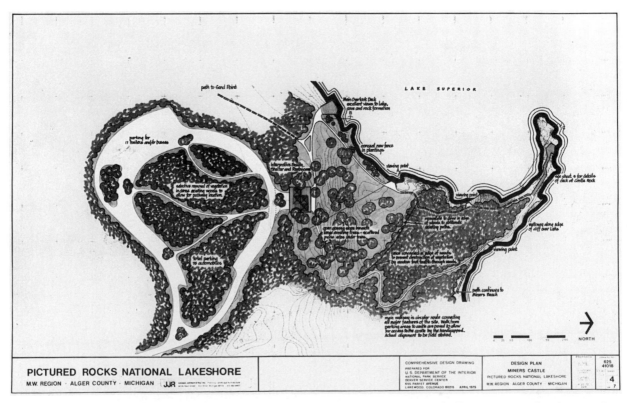

Overall plan of Miners Castle illustrates efforts to reduce visitor impact and allow increased volume of visitors. (Drawing courtesy Johnson, Johnson & Roy/inc.)

Visitor trampling of sandstone had badly eroded this popular attraction. (Photo courtesy Michigan Tourist Council)

This design solution has stopped further erosion, yet allows visitor access. (Photo courtesy Johnson, Johnson, & Roy/inc.)

# South Beach Park, Boca Raton, Florida

*Edward D. Stone, Jr. and Associates,*
*Landscape Architects*

The design of South Beach Park allows high-intensity access to the beach but also protects the very special character of the coastal ecosystem. Not only do the boardwalks prevent dune erosion, but they also educate the public about the necessity of resource protection. Indigenous plants have also been used effectively to stabilize the environment.

Boardwalk prevents erosion but provides access. (Photo courtesy Edward D. Stone, Jr. & Associates)

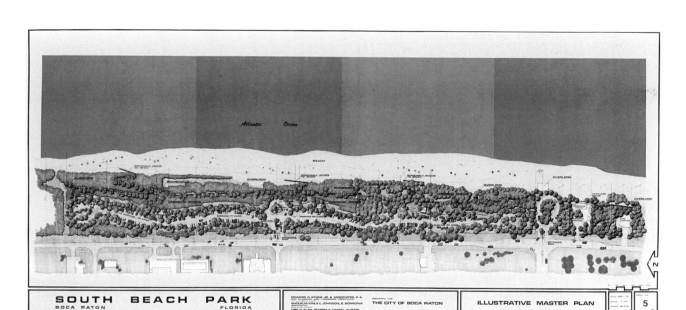

Plan of South Beach Park shows how park parallels Highway A1A, providing volume use as well as resource protection. (Plan courtesy Edward D. Stone, Jr. & Associates)

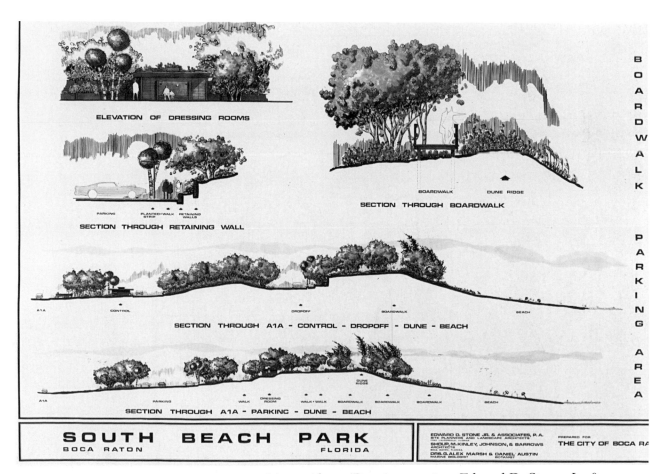

Sections show concepts for reclamation of dune ridges. (Drawing courtesy Edward D. Stone, Jr. & Associates)

# Woodland Park Zoological Gardens, Seattle, Washington

*Jones & Jones, Landscape Architects*

Zoos are important attractions for visitors, especially when they are designed as well as this. In Woodland Park, each exhibit, such as the African Savanna Exhibit and the Gorilla Exhibit, was located for best "fit" between the needed bioclimatic zone and the existing vegetation and microclimatic conditions. Further design considerations were geared toward the animals' welfare first and the visitors' second. This assured a more suitable habitat and enabled visitors to be immersed in the exhibit landscape. The designer's goal, executed with great skill, was to take people from their own backyards and "transport" them to exotic regions.

Visitors feel they are original discoverers of exotic animals. (Photo courtesy of Jones and Jones)

Plan of Woodland Park showing dominant animal habitat and ample public access. (Drawing courtesy Jones and Jones)

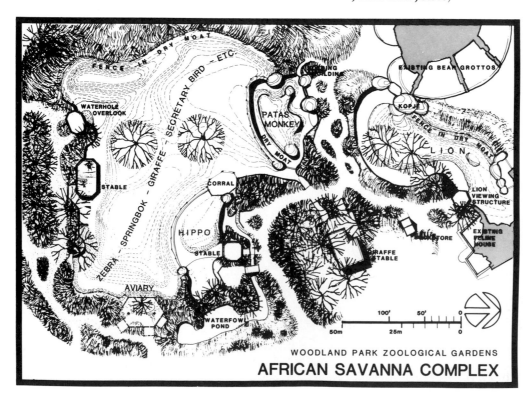

WOODLAND PARK ZOOLOGICAL GARDENS
**AFRICAN SAVANNA COMPLEX**

Landscape setting at access points sets the theme for exhibits. (Photo courtesy Jones and Jones)

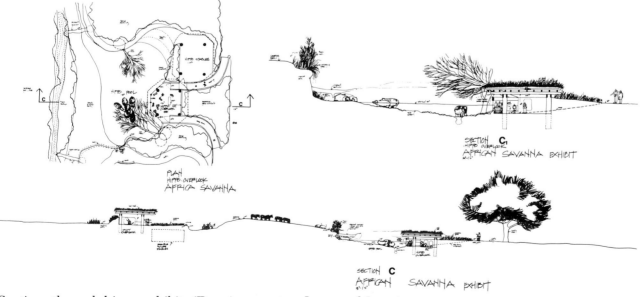

Sections through hippo exhibit. (Drawing courtesy Jones and Jones)

# Gas Works Park, Seattle, Washington

*Richard Haag Associates, Inc., Landscape Architects*

The designer's concept of retaining old gasworks in a public park, originally opposed both by city officials and the public, has now proven to be the centerpiece of an award-winning park design. The uncluttered views of the city and distant Cascade mountains have been retained. Original machinery, made safe for children to climb on, was painted in strong colors to stimulate their interest. An old boiler was fitted with a small stage and dance floor, demonstrating how imaginative design can reclaim abandoned industrial artifacts. It is now used by tourists as well as residents. The park also shows how effective a designer's catalytic role can be, bringing the several stakeholders together for a final design solution.

Plan of Gas Works Park shows creative design of open park space and waterfront as well as reuse of gas works. (Drawing courtesy Richard Haag Associates)

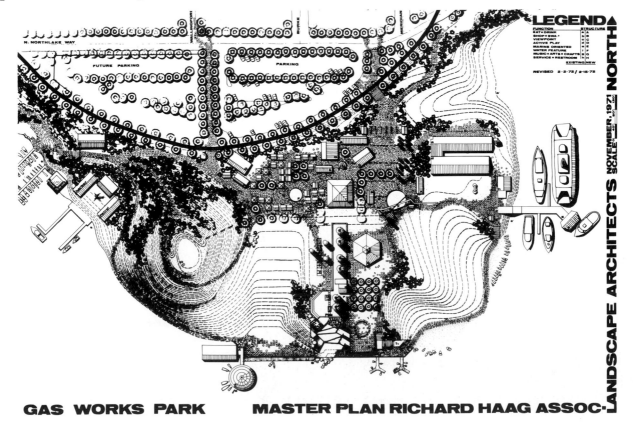

GAS WORKS PARK    MASTER PLAN RICHARD HAAG ASSOC.

Gas works structures and waterfront on Lake Union. (Photo courtesy Richard Haag Associates)

This park is a fun place for children, as well as educational for all. (Photo courtesy Richard Haag Associates)

# Jordan Pond House, Mt. Desert Island, Maine

*Woo & Williams, Architects; Landscape Architects*

Integrating public and private interests and blending site with building were the design challenges. This gateway facility within Acadia National Park, which has a restaurant, gift shop, and viewing areas, captures the essence of the old Jordan Pond House that burned down in 1979 and is enhanced by the natural beauty of its setting. The building was sited only after extensive shadow study and analysis of the surrounding environment were performed. The results convincingly demonstrate the designer's artistry, sensitivity to the environment, and integrative role.

Sketch of site development showing orientation of Jordan Pond House. (Drawing courtesy Woo & Williams)

Interiors include displays of historic artifacts. (Photo courtesy Woo & Williams)

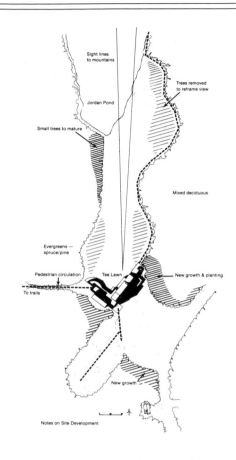

Original view of rebuilt Pond House is retained by protection of open space.
(Photo courtesy Woo & Williams)

# Punakaiki Visitor Centre, Greymouth, New Zealand

*Gary Hopkinson & Associates, Architects*

Because of its compatibility with the surrounding environment, this design has received many awards. The service center, which contains toilets, a kitchen, and recreational facilities, supplements the adjoining Dolomite Scenic Reserve, a major visitor attraction of the region. Nearby, in the Punakaiki Information Centre, displays, information, and an audiovisual presentation are integrated with a tearoom and souvenir shops for a functional attraction complex.

Simple, straightforward design of Information Center. (Photo courtesy Gary Hopkinson & Associates)

Harmonious camping facility nearby. (Photo courtesy Gary Hopkinson & Associates)

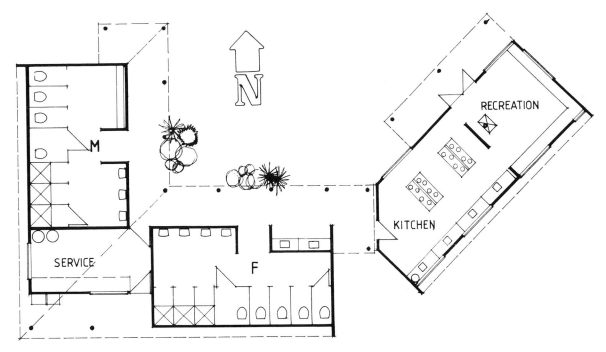

Plan of Punakaiki service center for Dolomite Scenic Reserve. (Drawing courtesy Gary Hopkinson & Associates)

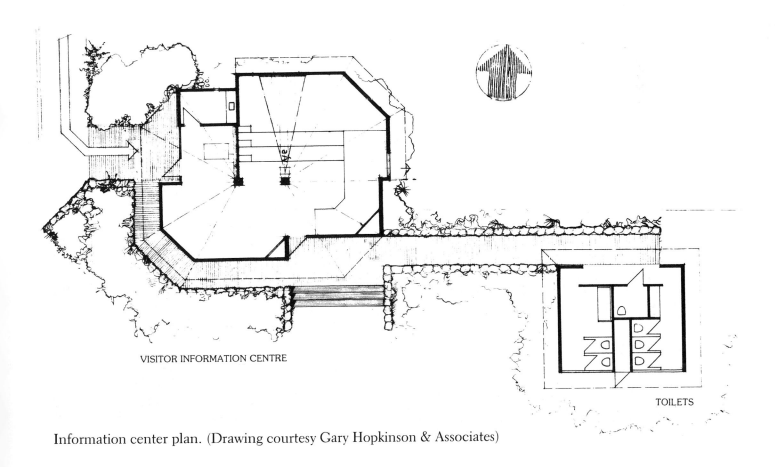

VISITOR INFORMATION CENTRE

TOILETS

Information center plan. (Drawing courtesy Gary Hopkinson & Associates)

# Giant's Causeway Centre, Belfast, Northern Ireland

*Andris Berzins, Architect; Robin Wade,*
*Interpretive designer*

This informative visitor center provides a more meaningful experience of the Giant's Causeway, a significant tourist attraction along Ireland's north coast, often called the Eighth Wonder of the World. The exterior design is appropriate to the barren basaltic headlands. The creative interior includes explanations and exhibits of the area's geology, personalized information, retail sales of literature and mementos, and descriptive audiovisual presentations.

Interior includes space for souvenir sales as well as educational exhibits. (Photo courtesy Andris Berzins)

Entrance approach to Giants Causeway visitor center. (Photo courtesy Andris Berzins)

Detail view of unusual geological spectacle along Irish coast. (Photo courtesy Andris Berzins)

# Brightleaf Square, Durham, North Carolina

*Ferebee, Walters & Associates, Architects*

Established downtowns can compete well with glitzy suburban shopping centers, particularly where there is creative redesign, new merchandising, and a mixture of tourists and residents. Originally built as tobacco factories, Brightleaf Square now retains the patina of an earlier era but provides intimate and distinctive shops, restaurants, and offices. Tourists can rediscover the warmth and pleasures of urban destinations when they are designed with such feeling as this.

View of redeveloped Brightleaf Square. (Photo courtesy Ferebee, Walters & Associates)

"Before" view of the blighted Brightleaf site. (Photo courtesy Ferebee, Walters & Associates)

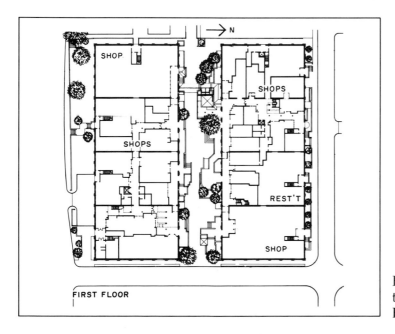

Plan of Brightleaf Square's restored tobacco factories. (Drawing courtesy Ferebee, Walters & Associates)

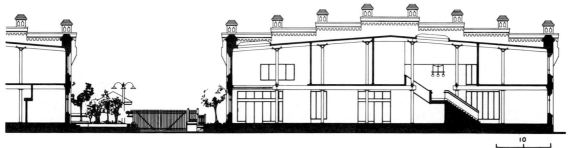

# Mary Rose Tudor Ship Museum, Portsmouth, England

*Andris Berzins & Associates, Architects*

A major repair, restoration, and conversion of an ancient timber-framed monument boathouse has produced an interesting focal point for visitors. This museum displays a sampling of the seventeen thousand artifacts recovered from the *Mary Rose*, a ship carrying seven hundred men and ninety-one guns that was ordered by King Henry VIII to play a key role in repelling a French invasion. Unfortunately for the English, as the ship set sail from Portsmouth in 1545, it was capsized by a gust of wind, and all but thirty of its men were lost. Remains of the hull were raised in 1982.

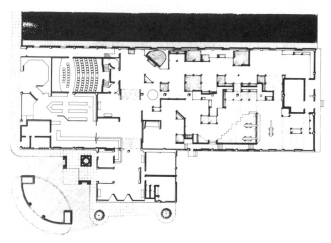

Plan of Mary Rose Tudor Ship Museum in ancient boathouse. (Drawing courtesy Andris Berzins)

View of interior with artifacts from the *Mary Rose*. (Photo: Martin Charles, courtesy Andris Berzins)

# Fort Mackinac, Mackinac Island, Michigan

*Eugene T. Petersen, Historic Restorer*

One of the first restorations not only to contain rebuilt authentic structures and historic artifacts but to provide dramatizations and interpretation for visitors is Fort Mackinac on a small island at the tip of Lake Huron. Thousands of visitors are attracted to the island annually because of its abundance of turn-of-the-century resort buildings, including the magnificent Grand Hotel, and because of its interesting nature and historic trails. The fort, with dramatizations of historic events, is the central feature of the destination. In order to avoid logistic problems of shipping and parking tourists cars and to preserve historic atmosphere, all cars are prohibited on the island.

This 4-square-mile (10-square-kilometer) island where Fort Mackinac is located played an important role, under French, British, and American flags, in the settlement of North America. (Drawing courtesy Mackinac Island State Park Commission)

Uniformed guides help interpret the many events of historic Fort Mackinac, now restored. (Photo courtesy Mackinac Island State Park Commission)

# Station Square, Pittsburgh, Pennsylvania

*Pittsburgh History and Landmarks
Foundation, Developers*

Part of a long-range revitalization of the Monongahela Riverfront, situated across from Pittsburgh's downtown core, Station Square is a 41-acre tract with obsolete and underutilized buildings dating from 1897 to 1917, owned by the Pittsburgh & Lake Erie Railroad. The old waiting room has been converted to a dining area; the old baggage room to a seafood and cocktail bar; the old dining room and ladies' waiting room to new dining areas; and an outdoor walkway to a dining area with a view of the downtown. Signage reflects the railroad theme. The entire complex is designed for maximum historic education and use.

One of several dining areas providing romantic and nostalgic atmosphere for visitors in a once-blighted area. (Photo courtesy Pittsburgh History and Landmarks Foundation)

Festive visitors enjoy the renovated Station Square area, complete with restored freight house on the right. (Photo courtesy Pittsburgh History and Landmarks Foundation)

# Durango-Silverton Narrow Gauge, Colorado

*Durango-Silverton Narrow Gauge R. R.,*
*Developers*

More than offering a trip back in time, this 45-mile restoration is a true attraction complex. It includes spectacular mountain scenery, old gold mines, diverse geological formations, and the flora and fauna of several life zones, as well as relics of old trains. The towns of Durango, Rockwood, Needleton, and Silverton are within the railway corridor and are representative of this frontier mining territory. Silverton and the Durango-Silverton narrow gauge D & RGW railroad have been designated as national historic landmarks by the National Park Service.

An example of a turn-of-the-century steam train attraction, this railroad passes through spectacular landscapes. (Photo courtesy Durango & Silverton Narrow Gauge RR)

# Signers Memorial, Washington, D. C.

*EDAW, Landscape Architects*

State and national shrines, such as the Memorial to the Signers of the Declaration of Independence, are of increasing significance to travelers. The designers sought to achieve a contemplative feeling that complemented the plants and lakes of Constitution Gardens. To prevent it from competing with the tall memorials that surrounded it, the designers kept the Signers Memorial low and horizontal. This decision reflected both close cooperation between the designers and the client (the National Park Service) and sensitivity to visitors.

The design, which was intentionally kept low, offers a dignified and harmonious solution for a national visitor shrine. (Photo: Maxwell MacKenzie)

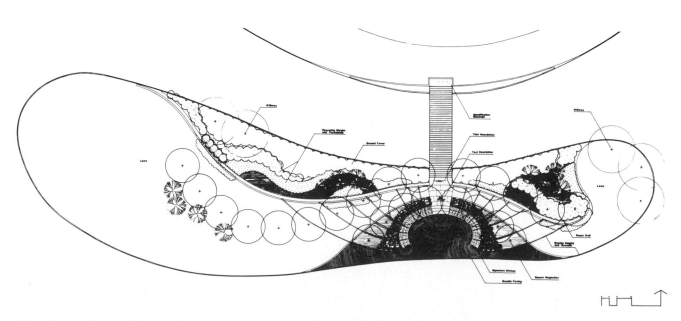

The finely designed Signers Memorial, constructed from fifty-six pink granite blocks, is neat and classical. (Drawing courtesy EDAW)

# Great Wall Sheraton Hotel, Beijing, People's Republic of China

*The Becket Group, Architects*

Modeled after the trend-setting Dallas Hyatt Regency, also designed by Becket, this hotel demanded special structural design as well as functional and aesthetic adaptation to another culture. The prevalence of earthquakes mandated special steel and welding for structural functionalism. Innovations (for a hotel in China) included a reflective glass exterior, 24-hour room service, a child-care center, a computerized room status and reservation system, a nightclub, and an underground garage. Site amenities include waterfalls, reflecting pools, and an uncluttered setting.

Striking design of Great Wall Sheraton Hotel in a pleasant landscape setting. (Photo courtesy Welton Becket Associates)

# Mill Creek Restoration and Visitor Center, Mackinaw City, Cheboygan, Michigan

*Victor Hogg, Interpretive Designer*

After intensive land analysis and archaeological study, the 1780 sawmill was rebuilt on its original site. Reconstructed houses, dam, fish ladder, and an Indian camp round out the display. In the visitor center, interpretation of natural resources, and how man has used them from the Ice Age to the present, offers tourists an educational as well as an entertaining experience.

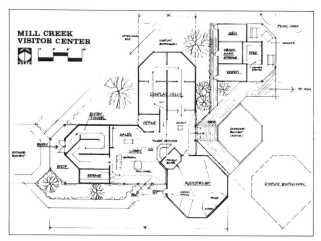

Plan of Mill Creek visitor center, housing displays and other interpretive aids. (Photo courtesy Mackinac Island State Park Commission)

Sketch plan of Mill Creek restoration complex, simulating the 1780 structures. (Drawing by Victor R. Nelhiebel)

Visitors now gain an understanding of how this early mill was located and operated. (Photo courtesy Mackinac Island State Park Commission)

Visitors learning about mill operations from interpreter. (Photo courtesy Mackinac Island State Park Commission)

# South Street Seaport, New York City

*Clarke & Rapuano, Inc., Landscape
Architects; Dean Abbott, Designer*

A redesigned waterfront and streetscape that captures the feeling of the historic Fulton Fish Market and shipping port. Attractions for visitors include markets, specialty foods, restaurants, crafts, a museum, and views of historic ships, Brooklyn Bridge, and river traffic. A colorful demonstration of integrated and collaborative design of public and private reuse for tourists and residents. Clarke & Rapuano collaborated closely with Benjamin Thompson Associates, the Eggers Group, P. C., and New York City clients to create a distinct sense of place.

Plan of waterfront development showing Museum Pier and restored market buildings. (Photo courtesy Clarke & Rapuano Inc.)

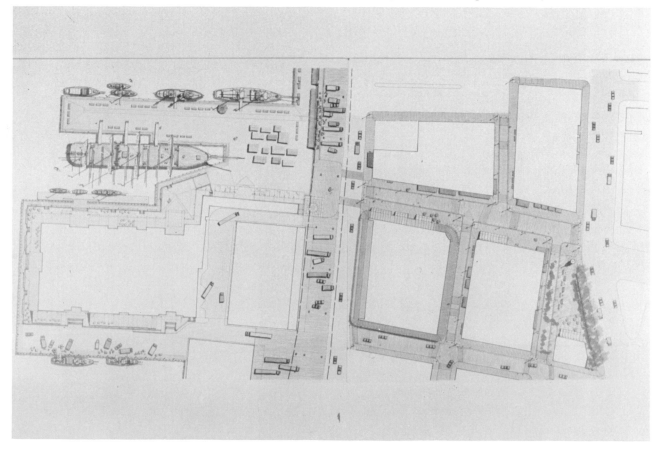

View of South Street Seaport from Pier 17, showing U.S. Coast Guard bark, *Eagle*. (Photo: Dean Abbott)

Visitors enjoying the rehabilitated shops; restored 1811 Schermerhorn block in background. (Photo: James Coleman)

# Polynesian Village Hotel, Walt Disney World, Orlando, Florida

*Welton Becket Associates, Architects*

Responding to travel-market segmentation, the Polynesian Village Hotel provides a scintillating break from the monotony of many hotel offerings. Although it has five hundred rooms, the hotel seems much smaller and more intimate because of its low profile, forty-acre coverage, and delightful landscape design. Although cased in thematic wood, the basic construction is steel, built as separate modules and trucked to the site.

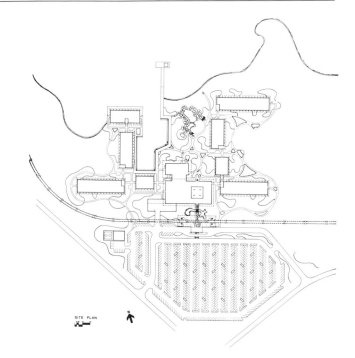

Site plan of Polynesian Village Hotel. (Photo courtesy Welton Becket Associates)

Restful tropical setting for resort hotel adjacent to attractions of Walt Disney World. (Photo: Balthazar Korab)

# Jackson Brewery Development, New Orleans, Louisiana

*Concordia, Architects; Landesign, Landscape Architects*

The renovated Jackson Brewery is an excellent example of historic reuse. It is part of the attraction complex, the French Quarter, within the destination zone of New Orleans and vicinity. Originally built in 1891, this landmark was reopened in 1984 after having been closed for ten years. The design challenge, well met, was to comply with the stipulations of the Department of the Interior for historic restoration, with the regulations of the Vieux Carré Commission (the local preservation body), and with the needs of visitors in a shopping-entertainment complex. The architecture reflects the Romanesque origins and yet sparkles with contemporary appeal. This festive redevelopment contains six floors of shops, restaurants, and craft stores, as well as spectacular views of the Mississippi River waterfront and the French Quarter.

First-phase redevelopment, adjacent to Jackson Square, French Quarter, New Orleans. (Photos courtesy Jackson Brewery Development Corporation)

THE JACKSON BREWERY DEVELOPMENT    New Orleans, Louisiana
CONCORDIA
Architects    LANDESIGN
Landscape Architects

Sketch of market complex attraction developed from defunct brewery. (Drawing courtesy Jackson Brewery Development Corporation)

# Ponderosa Lodge, Mount Hermon, California

*Johnson, Johnson & Roy/inc., Landscape Architects*

Ponderosa Lodge is an astute and ecologically sound design solution to a difficult task—placing a young adult and teenage religious conference facility on a fragile mountainside. Close collaboration convinced the owner to eliminate several intensive land-use aspects of the program and protect much of the site as a nature preserve. The natural environment of the site dictated the size and intensity of development. The lodge was carefully located on a gentle slope, where intensive use has least impact. Automobiles are stored on the perimeter of the site, so that the natural beauty is in no way diminished. Views to the Pacific Ocean, canopies of live oak and madrone trees, and dense shade from redwoods were assets of considerable importance in siting all structures. All building design is sensitive to the rustic setting.

Plan of Ponderosa Lodge conference area development, with buildings sited to protect landscape assets. (Drawing courtesy Johnson, Johnson & Roy/inc.)

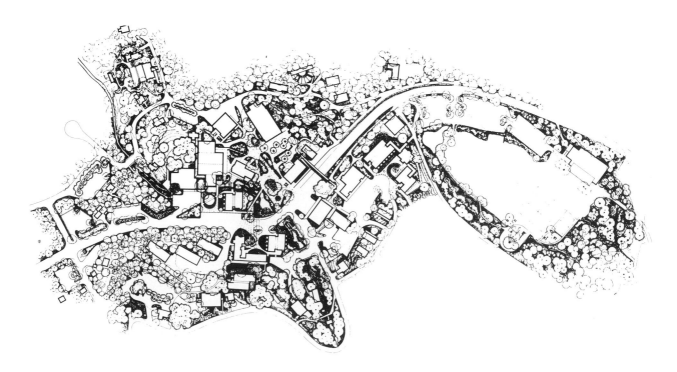

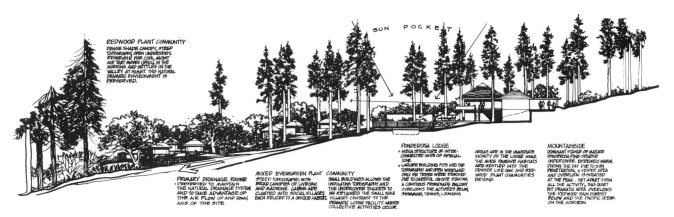

Plan of Ponderosa Lodge site. (Drawing courtesy Johnson, Johnson & Roy/inc.)

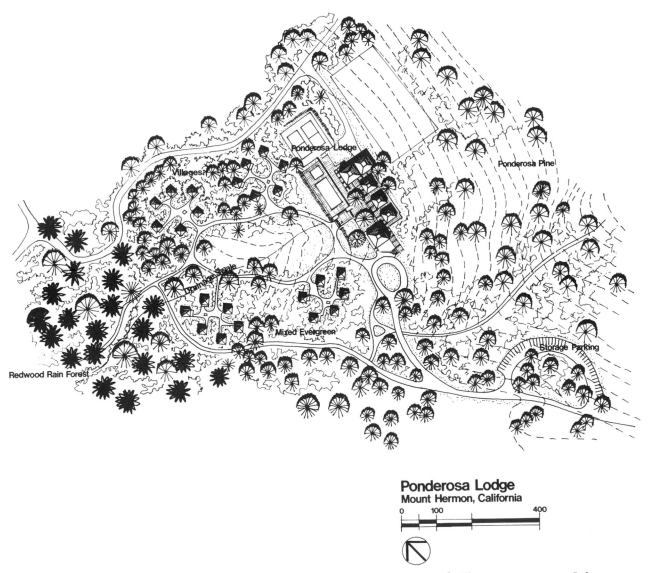

One of many studies made to make sure environmental assets are protected. (Drawing courtesy Johnson, Johnson & Roy/inc.)

Sketch of Ponderosa Lodge, for communication with client. (Drawing courtesy Johnson, Johnson & Roy/ inc.)

View of completed Ponderosa Lodge showing unusual protection of natural resources. (Photo courtesy Johnson, Johnson & Roy/inc.)

Hard surfaces are kept to a minimum in all development, to protect the environment. (Photo courtesy Johnson, Johnson & Roy/inc.)

# The Waterside, Norfolk, Virginia

*Wallace Roberts and Todd, Architects,*
*Landscape Architects*

This project illustrates the integrative role of designers. The architects and landscape architects involved first worked with the city of Norfolk to create the Downtown 1990 Plan, which provided long-range guidance for revitalization and future development for visitors as well as residents. Then, several projects, including the Waterside, were planned for collaborative public and private development of this busy waterfront. The Waterside is a pleasant shopping, eating, and entertainment attraction. It includes space and facilities for five restaurants, twenty-two fast food enterprises, thirty-five specialty retail and market produce shops, thirty-four kiosks, and eighteen pushcart vendors.

Downtown Norfolk 1990 Plan identifying overall projected revitalization of the entire area. (Drawing courtesy Wallace Roberts and Todd)

Creative redevelopment of harbor waterscape and architecture has added vitality and purpose for visitors and residents. (Photo: Bruce A. Tamte, courtesy Wallace Roberts and Todd)

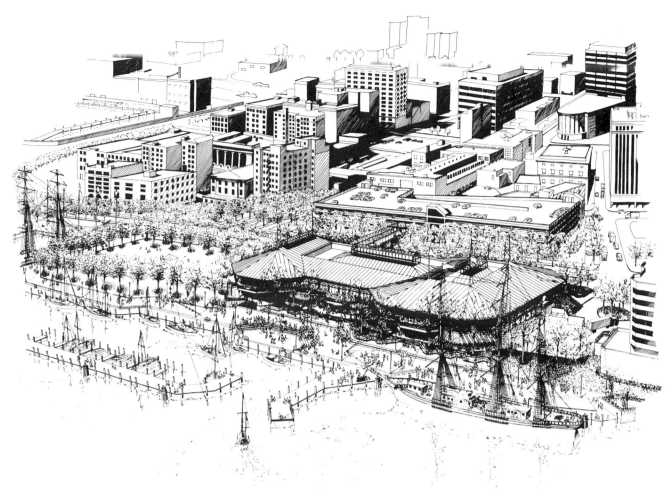

Detail plan of Waterside project showing relationship of harbor and waterfront structures. (Drawing courtesy Wallace Roberts and Todd)

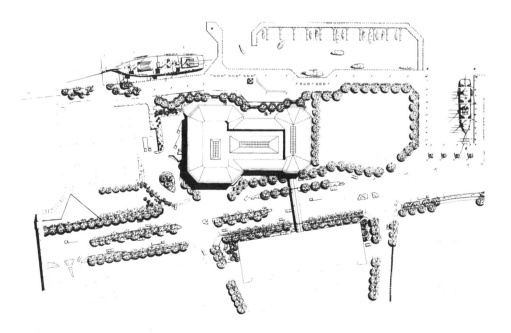

Sketch plan of redevelopment of the Waterside project area. (Drawing courtesy Wallace Roberts and Todd)

# Jupiters Casino, Broadbeach Island, Queensland, Australia

*Sprankle, Lynd & Sprague, Architects*

This exceptional design complex, intimately linked with a 622-room Conrad Hilton International Hotel, illustrates travel services integrated with an attraction complex. The interior design is not only sensitive to activities within but maximizes sweeping views of the gardens, Pacific Ocean, and hinterland mountain ranges. The complex includes a wide array of destination attractions, such as a discotheque, a convention center, tennis courts, a swimming complex, and outdoor entertainment areas.

A garden atrium forms a link between hotel and casino. A translucent canopy ties the rectangular hotel design to the "boomerang-shaped" casino. (Photo: Chris Pilz, courtesy Sprankle, Lynd & Sprague)

# Beach House, Moultonboro, New Hampshire

*Matarazzo Design, Landscape Architects*

This award-winning vacation home design proves that tourism can respect resource settings while providing recreational enjoyment. The plan resists ice movement in winter, serves several boat sizes, makes little impact on the environment, and yet provides an attractive outdoor living space. The recessed design maintains the integrity of the original shoreline. Because of its high quality, this design has served as a prototype for sensitive waterfront development throughout the Lake Winnipesaukee area.

Environmental integrity dominated all design decisions for this resort setting. (Photo courtesy Matarazzo Design)

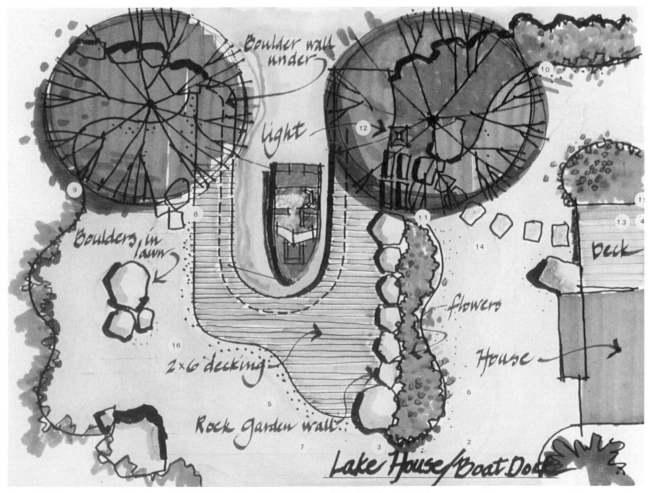

Beach House plan shows recessed boat well, decking, and outdoor living room. (Drawing courtesy Matarazzo Design)

# Windward Harbor, Center Harbor, New Hampshire

*Matarazzo Design, Landscape Architects;*
*Claude Miquelle and Associates,*
*Architects*

Environmentally sensitive designers have created a functional and idyllic 46-acre plan for this complex of waterfront vacation homes. New design has been keyed to the turn-of-the-century boathouse. The beach, marina, and pine forest offer enticing on-site uses. The location provides easy access to a larger complex, which includes the White Mountains, lakes, streams, and Alpine ski trails.

Overview sketch of Windward Harbor resort complex with wooded cottage setting surrounding the old boathouse. (Drawing courtesy Matarazzo Design)

View of cottages and remodeled boathouse in foreground. (Photo: Cymie Payne)

# Bal Harbour Shops, Bal Harbour, Florida

*Bozas & Pirich, Landscape Architects*

Proof that the approach from parking to prestigious shops need not be barren and hostile is this converted gas station site adjacent to stores in Bal Harbour. The award-winning landscape design incorporated plant materials of a kind and scale that dominated the original shopping area. As tourists seek more shopping outlets, areas such as this will become attractions unto themselves.

Landscape detail of foreground is essential to the quality of shopping for residents as well as visitors. (Photo courtesy Bal Harbour Shops)

Attractive approach to Bal Harbour shops was once an ugly gasoline service station. (Photo courtesy Bal Harbour Shops)

# Fiddler's Green Amphitheatre, Englewood, Colorado

*Hargreaves Associates, Landscape Architects*

An award jury's comment: "Part of a new process of educating clientele to use projects to make connection with the community. Done with verve and gusto. Magic making—a special place for special happenings."[4] An open theater for the performing arts, this dramatic landscape attraction has promise of becoming a destination point for visitors as well as residents.

Festival performance in process, with innovative stage backdrop. (Photo courtesy Hargreaves Associates)

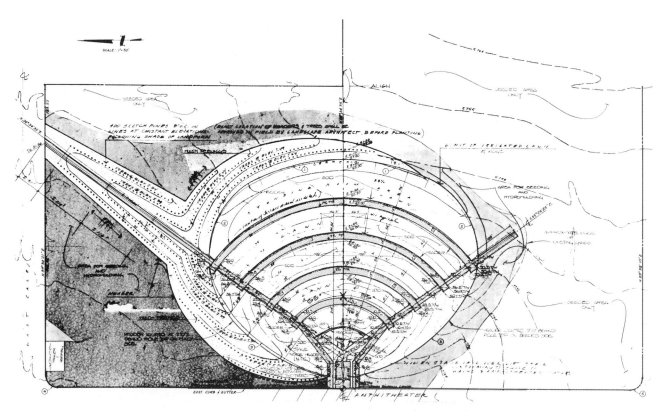

Plan of Fiddler's Green, an unusual outdoor theater, indicating contours for reshaping the land. (Drawing courtesy Hargreaves Associates)

# Scenic Tour Barge, Paris, France

*Salt and Pepper Tours, developers*

Waterways are increasingly popular for tourism because they offer an experience unequalled by any other attraction form. Simply by fitting out barges to accommodate visitors, designers enable small groups to be enriched by the waterfront landscape of rivers and canals throughout Europe, at low cost.

Casual interior of tour barge provides for private relaxing as well as viewing of scenic river corridor. (Photo courtesy Salt and Pepper Tours)

*La Patache Eautobus* (tour barge) on the St. Martin Canal, Paris. (Photo courtesy Salt and Pepper Tours)

# Infomart, Dallas, Texas

*Growald & Associates, Architects*

Called the world's first information processing market center, this innovative design allows many computer and telecommunications manufacturers to display their products. As a center for displays, meetings, conferences, and receptions, it provides an important information link for trade elsewhere in normal retail outlets. Reflecting the increased sophistication of business and trade travel attactions, the building was inspired by London's Crystal Palace and contains 1.5 million square feet of space.

Interior view of central reception lobby leading to market areas. (Photo courtesy Dallas Market Center Company)

Elevation drawing of Infomart facade, reminisicent of London's Crystal Palace. (Drawing courtesy Dallas Market Center Company)

Finished building, housing an entirely new concept in marketing. (Photo courtesy Dallas Market Center Company)

Entrance with vaulted ribs sets the theme for the fantasy world to come. (Photo: Matt Wargo, courtesy Venturi, Rauch and Scott Brown)

# Shangri-La Hotel, Singapore, Republic of Singapore

*Belt, Collins & Associates, Landscape Architects; Wimberly, Whisenand, Allison, Tong & Goo, Ltd., Architects*

Designed as a contrast to the British colonial style that dominates the island, this hotel and site offer an oasis in an intensive urban environment. Collaboration among owners, architects, and landscape architects has produced a functional service business for tourists that also makes a striking design statement. The site is studied by professional and student landscape architects for its excellence of design. Even indigenous populations have gained a new appreciation for the beauty of the local flora. The development has been dubbed a "controlled jungle."

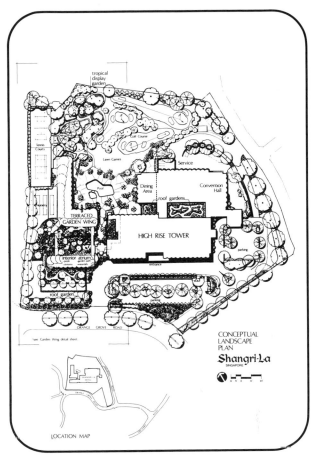

Site plan for the Shangri-La Hotel shows gardens inserted into a dense urban setting. (Drawing courtesy Belt, Collins & Associates)

View of hotel and site demonstrates care in incorporating a restful landscape setting into a major hotel complex. (Photo courtesy Belt, Collins & Associates)

# West Edmonton Mall, Edmonton, Alberta, Canada

*Triple Five Corporation, Developers*

Called a megamall, this is one of the most massive shopping and entertainment complexes ever built. The 5.2 million-square-foot development contains a skating rink, marine theater, roller coaster, lake with submarines, video arcade, petting zoo, thirteen fountains, twenty theaters, 135 eating places, and 828 stores. A major tourist attraction in Canada, the mall draws 400,000 visitors a week, most from out of town. A shuttle bus connects this huge attraction with eleven hotels.

Swimming pool and a sample of the many fun facilities. (Photo courtesy West Edmonton Mall and Travel Alberta)

Aerial view of West Edmonton Mall entertainment and shopping complex. (Rendering courtesy West Edmonton Mall and Travel Alberta)

Pleasant outdoor-like interior is surrounded by shops. (Photo courtesy West Edmonton Mall and Travel Alberta)

# PGA National Resort, Palm Beach Gardens, Florida

*Schwab & Twitty, Inc., Architects, Urban Design, Inc., Landscape Architects*

This four-square-mile destination attraction complex consists of several types of housing and services surrounding four championship golf courses. Responding to a market trend of retirees seeking golf, this design maximizes exposure to freeway frontage yet provides ample privacy. Intensity of housing varies. The complex includes a hotel, restaurants, a swimming pool, tennis courts, a fitness center, and a dance studio. A series of lakes, canals, and weir structures protect ground-water levels to minimize salt water intrusion. Housing design in separate neighborhoods is varied, but the golf course setting retains harmony throughout.

Plan for four-square-mile major destination resort complex. (Drawing courtesy Urban Design, Inc.)

Four championship golf courses form the centerpiece of the resort. (Photo courtesy PGA National Resort)

Many recreational opportunities are available, including swimming. (Photo courtesy PGA National Resort)

# Albert Street Revitalization, Winnipeg, Manitoba

*Hilderman Witty Crosby Hanna & Associates, Landscape Architects*

The first streetscaping project in the Old Market Square District of Winnipeg, Albert Street has set the character for the entire district's restoration. Street parking continues, but new pedestrian bays reach into former travelways, increasing the attractiveness of the area and the efficiency with which people use it. The designer has used interlocking pavers, concrete headers, brick-and-trim half circles, antique-styled bollards, benches, and simulated period light standards to complement the restoration of the historic building facades. The City Council Committee on the Environment coordinates design for all redevelopment in the district.

Renovated hotel entrance illustrates design details of paving, curb, bollards, and planters. (Photo courtesy Hilderman Witty Crosby Hanna & Associates)

General view of Market Square district shows planters, pedestrian plaza, and period-style lamp standards. (Photo courtesy Hilderman Witty Crosby Hanna & Associates)

# Mauna Lani Resort, South Kohala, Hawaii

*Belt, Collins & Associates, Landscape
Architects*

This outstanding award-winning design exem-
plifies the fulfillment of all tourism development goals: it stimulates business, is sensitive
to the environment, and meets market needs.
Because of their archaeological and historical
values, prehistoric Kalahuipua'a fish ponds
and historic sites have been kept in preserves.
The 351-room Mauna Lani hotel and private
homes (Mauna Lani Terrace) have been sited
to protect these preserves and maintain aesthetic vistas to the ocean and mountains. The
area also includes the well-designed Francis
H. I'i Brown Golf Course. The rugged natural
beauty of the volcanic landscape has been retained with skill. New native plantings, as well
as a six-story atrium within the hotel, enhance
the site.

Master plan for the Mauna Lani resort complex
shows restraint in access, thus protecting site
assets and yet incorporating quality resort
development. (Drawing courtesy Belt, Collins &
Associates)

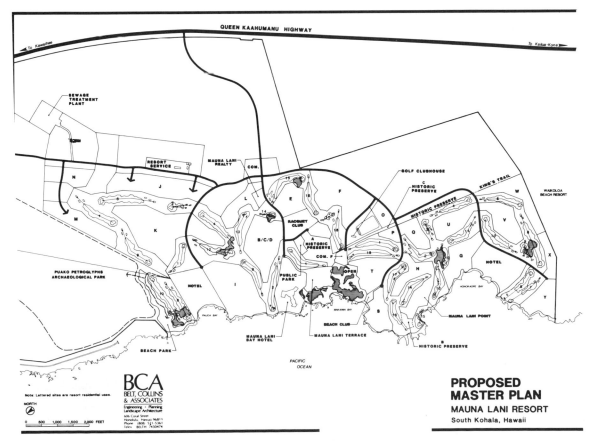

**PROPOSED
MASTER PLAN**
MAUNA LANI RESORT
South Kohala, Hawaii

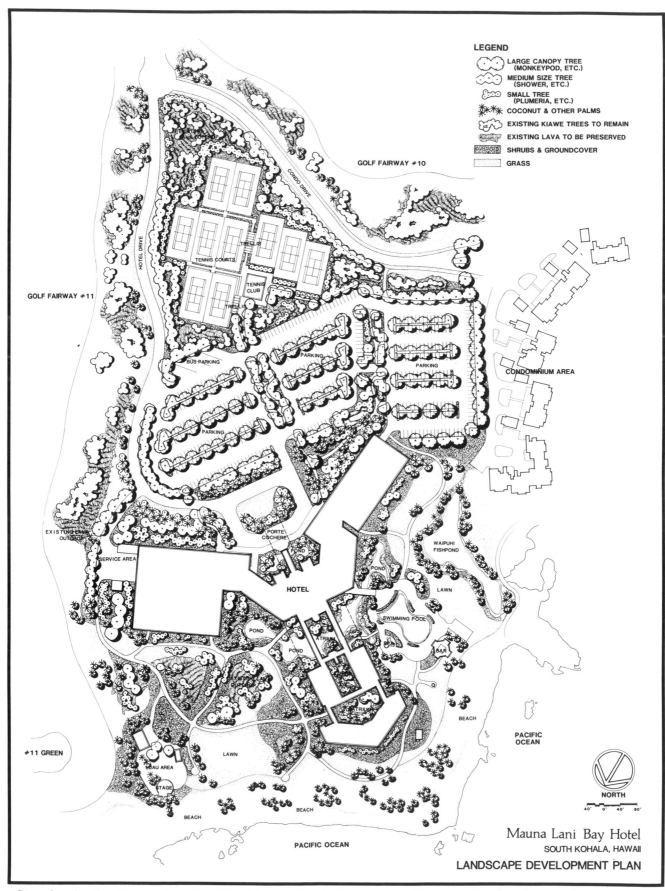

**LEGEND**

- LARGE CANOPY TREE (MONKEYPOD, ETC.)
- MEDIUM SIZE TREE (SHOWER, ETC.)
- SMALL TREE (PLUMERIA, ETC.)
- COCONUT & OTHER PALMS
- EXISTING KIAWE TREES TO REMAIN
- EXISTING LAVA TO BE PRESERVED
- SHRUBS & GROUNDCOVER
- GRASS

GOLF FAIRWAY #10

GOLF FAIRWAY #11

TENNIS COURTS

TRELLIS

TENNIS CLUB

TRELLIS

HOTEL DRIVE

CONDO DRIVE

CONDOMINIUM AREA

BUS PARKING

PARKING

PARKING

PARKING

EXISTING

SERVICE AREA

PORTE COCHERE

POND

POND

WAIPUHI FISHPOND

LAWN

HOTEL

POND

POND

ATRIUM

SWIMMING POOL

BAR

BEACH

POND

ATRIUM

PACIFIC OCEAN

#11 GREEN

LUAU AREA

STAGE

LAWN

BEACH

BEACH

BEACH

PACIFIC OCEAN

NORTH

40'  0'  40'  80'

Mauna Lani Bay Hotel
SOUTH KOHALA, HAWAII

LANDSCAPE DEVELOPMENT PLAN

Site plan for the Mauna Lani Bay Hotel is sensitive to land assets of topography and vistas to the ocean. (Drawing courtesy Belt, Collins & Associates)

View of completed hotel reveals design creativity both in orientation and utilization of site. (Photo courtesy Belt, Collins & Associates)

# Parador Nacional de Siguenza, Siguenza, Spain

*Secretariat of State for Tourism,
Developers*

Few countries have engaged in historic adaptive reuse for tourism better than Spain, with its many *paradores*. These inns are converted castles, palaces, and convents that retain the basic traditions of past centuries but have modern hotel conveniences. An example is the Parador Nacional "Castilla de Siguenza," located 128 kilometers from Madrid and converted to a large hotel in the 1970s. *Paradores*, which are located in small towns or rural areas throughout the country, offer a rich travel experience not available in the more standardized hotels of Spain's large cities.

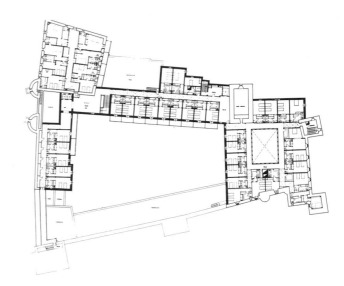

Plan showing remodeling of second floor into guest rooms. (Drawing courtesy Secretariat of State for Tourism, Spain)

The ancient Castilla de Siguenza is now converted to tourist lodging. (Photo courtesy Secretariat of State for Tourism, Spain)

Interior courtyard of the old castle has been modified very little. (Photo courtesy Secretariat of State for Tourism, Spain)

# 10/

# Epilogue

Vacationscape, the art and practice of integrated design and development for travel, demands a greater commitment toward better quality. The *descriptions* and *prescriptions* offered here are less concerned with the statistical than the creative. When one reflects on the new talent emerging in the design and development fields, one hopes that a greater share will be directed toward better tourism environments.

Just as a painting begins with canvas, paint, and artist and ends with beholder, the travel environment begins with land, developer, and designer and ends with establishments for the traveler's use and enrichment. Economic, social, and personal gains can accrue through application of the principles and concepts of vacationscape. This is not utopian. It is practical politics, good economics, and sound cultural and environmental development.

Vacationscape seeks to defuse the polarized and often volatile positions of preservation versus development that have so greatly inhibited progress in tourism and resource protection. More and more, designers and developers are discovering that these ideologies are not only compatible but, in reality, symbiotic. Protection of resources is essential to the develop-

ment of tourism. But there is yet work to be done. Protectionists, for example, as advocates of national parks, are still not convinced that visitor services are as essential as resources. On the other hand, the business sector has not yet fully supported resource protection as essential to much of tourist business. As designers accept the challenge inherent in this polarity and exercise a stronger catalytic role, greater integration will follow.

Lest the reader conclude that vacationscape calls for a high-power directive, nothing could be farther from the intent. Vacationscape is in concert with the belief that decisions have greater value when they are made by many rather than by a few. The problems and issues related here will be resolved more readily and effectively by a multitude of decision makers than by a centralized authority. The fundamentals of a market economy and free enterprise are compatible with vacationscape: private property, economic freedom, economic incentives, competitive markets, and a limited role of government.[1]

When property is in the hands of many and the consequences of ownership are tied to decisions, those decisions are likely to be better ones. However, when property is owned by the public, nobody seems to care whether it is adequately protected and managed. One obvious

*Gasparilla* invasion. (Photo courtesy Tampa News Bureau)

195

example is that people litter their homes far less than they do public highways and parks. Bureaucracies are too remote from the land to design, develop, and manage it well both for resource protection and visitor use.

Responding to market trends rather than to governmental directives is a more efficient way of providing travelers with what they need and desire. With economic freedom, that is, without quotas or mandates regarding size, number, quality, and price, the market is the best modulator for development. Designers could well improve their understanding of markets.

Economic incentives encourage entrepreneurs and workers to meet new as well as existing needs. Higher-quality services and products for travelers must be offered if business revenues are to be enjoyed.

Of course, competition can meet the demands from the diversity of markets most effectively. Competition among many decision makers provides the best quality at the best price.

There is no question about the need for governmental health and safety regulations. But excessive intervention by government can strangle the effective operation of free enterprise. In the United States, airline deregulation has resulted in generally better service at lower rates. Likewise, under free enterprise professional designers, investors, and developers have a great opportunity to create the very best vacationscape.

Governments, however, should play an important nonintervening role in market economies. Such a role could encompass several functions that would foster, not inhibit, the development of free enterprise and better design. One function is the integration of state, provincial, and federal agency policies for tourism design and development, because decisions by highway, recreation, park, historic and tourism departments impinge on tourism but are seldom coordinated. Outdoor recreation, for example, is very important to tourism and yet policies and practices of outdoor recreation agencies are seldom coordinated with those of tourism. Another area of cooperation between governments and the private sector is

the analysis and reporting of basic information on market trends and resource potential throughout a region. This aid to all decision makers and designers, especially if annual, could greatly improve the process of development. Moreover, governments could offer certain incentives for business development in the most appropriate locations. The success of the Main Street programs in the United States and Canada testify to the effectiveness of this role. Finally, governments could foster vacationscape through greater support of education and research. The very young need to be taught how to travel as much as they need to be taught about travel careers. Vocational and higher education in the fundamentals of tourism could produce a population with much greater awareness of the many facets of travel and a desire for better tourism environments. Research into design issues and problems must complement the creative training of design professionals.

Vacationscape requires greater awareness and application of planning and design fundamentals. Hoteliers, for example, have demonstrated great improvements in internal business recently. Yet to come, however, is sufficient recognition of the personal as well as social advantages of greater *integration* with other components of tourism. Hoteliers are removed from parks, historic sites, theme parks, and convention centers only by the distance to the nearest guest. When hoteliers and designers are party to decisions on attractions and transportation, they will increase their revenues and more completely satisfy the needs of travelers.

The principles of vacationscape imply a much stronger community role. In the popular view, tourism is the responsibility solely of travel promoters and hoteliers. Vacationscape shows how complex tourism really is. It penetrates virtually every aspect of community life. Tourists increasingly seek the amenities of communities. Although they may traverse the hinterland throughout portions of their travel, all tourists are sooner or later brought to communities. Communities are not only logical focal points for travel services, they often contain the greatest potential for the development of attractions.

But tourism development from the community perspective meets many obstacles.[2] The business sector is usually supportive, but others may not be. Small and medium-size communities often repeat the poor design and management seen elsewhere. Local residents see tourism as a threat to their traditional quality of life, because much of it is accomplished by outsiders and out of their control. They fear three kinds of negative effects: social, environmental, and economic.[3] Vacationscape, which emphasizes strong catalytic leadership by designers, can mitigate all these concerns. Nearly all of the decisions made by communities in the interest of residents have important implications for tourism. But, until these decisions overtly address the welfare of visitors as well as residents, tourism will continue to be treated cosmetically.

Vacationscape also requires a special emphasis on transportation. Air passengers are already responding favorably to travel packages that include lodging, attractions, and ground transportation. As greater and greater concern over the total environment is shown, air travel, as a segment of the whole, will take on even greater meaning. Air travel businesses will find greater success from application of the principles and concepts of vacationscape than from changes in technology.

For highway designers and decision makers the principles of vacationscape can foster highways that have greater public value. When engineers are preoccupied with the technical side of highway building, the traveler's perspective is often neglected. The concept of "blue highways,"[4] or infrequently traveled rural roads that often offer interesting experiences, shows the importance of a more comprehensive and personal highway policy.

Tourist promoters have a point when they state that nearly every community can have tourism if it is promoted heavily enough. But this is valid only insofar as the community has something to promote. Implicit in vacationscape is the product side, especially as it relates to particular places and the development of indigenous attractions. The product side of tourism offers the greatest challenge today for the designer to create settings, facilities, and services of interest to visitors. Then, and only then, is a community worthy of promotion.

Threaded through all the axioms of vacationscape is the need for integration. If tourism is to function more smoothly as a system, the many parts need to be refitted and tuned to complement one another. Planning and design are obvious ways of making this happen. But too often plans and designs are considered products rather than processes. Development is not merely so many buildings, sites, and structures:

> Development is a process of learning, adaptation and purposeful change capable of releasing new potentials. And development is a *capacity*, defined by what people and communities can do with what they have to improve the quality of their lives.[5]

Incumbent upon modern man as creator of the vacationscape is a moral responsibility. Years ago restraints on development were many because we could not build skyscrapers, jet planes, and controlled interior climates. Until the social reversals of the 1960s the primary question was, *Can we do it?* Science and technology offered new ways to build more, bigger, and faster. Now, the question of *whether* we *should* do it is becoming more important. As communities, states, provinces, and nations rush to develop tourism, the question of whether it should be done needs to be asked more frequently. Decision makers need to temper their zeal with restraint so that potential negative impacts can be avoided. The thesis of this book is that better design and management can aid greatly in solving many tourism problems. But there is a point at which society may wish to decide it does not want more tourism. Perhaps it will want only better tourism, or perhaps it will want none at all.

In any case, the designer's role as integrator, leader, and facilitator, as well as innovator, will ensure that magnum leap from a process of merely muddling through to more effective collaborative action.

# Notes

### Chapter 1. Toward New Tourism Environments

1. Alister Mathieson and Geoffrey Wall, *Tourism—Economic, Physical, and Social Impacts* (London: Longman, 1982), 186.
2. Geoffrey Alan Jellicoe, "The Search for a Paradise Garden," *IFLA Yearbook 1985/86, Hong Kong, Hungary, Cairo,* International Federation of Landscape Architects (Versailles, France: IFLA, 1986), 6.

### Chapter 2. Tourism Myopia

1. David Lowenthal and Hugh C. Prince, "English Landscape Tastes," *Geographical Review* 55, no. 2 (April 1955): 82
2. Hans Friedrich Werkmeister, "The 'Perfect Way' to Tut-Ank-Amun," *IFLA Yearbook 1985/86, Hong Kong, Hungary, Cairo,* International Federation of Landscape Architects (Versailles, France: IFLA, 1986), 182.
3. Tom McMillan, *Tourism Tomorrow: Towards a Canadian Tourism Strategy* (Ottawa, Canada: Tourism Canada, 1985), 79.
4. Adolf Schmitt, "Cairo Seminar: Summary," *IFLA Yearbook 1985/86, Hong Kong, Hungary, Cairo,* International Federation of Landscape Architects (Versailles, France: IFLA, 1986), 158.
5. Edward T. McMahon, "Opinion," *Place* 4, no. 10 (November 1984): 8.
6. Werkmeister, "The 'Perfect Way,' " 182.
7. Jerome Turler, *The Traveiler* (Gainesville, Florida: Scholar's Facsimiles & Reprints, 1951), 5.
8. Ronald C. Sheck, Director, Planning and Development, State of New Mexico Transportation Department. Letter to author, 19 August 1986.
9. Grant W. Sharpe, *Interpreting the Environment* (New York: Wiley, 1976), 3.
10. Edward T. McMahon, "Saving Landmarks, Losing Our Landscape," *Preservation News,* March 1985.

### Chapter 3. Travelers, Public Involvement, and Design

1. Hans Huth, *Nature and the American: Three Centuries of Changing Attitudes* (Berkeley: University of California Press, 1957), 5.
2. Foster Rhea Dulles, A *History of Recreation: America Learns to Play,* 2nd ed., rev. (New York: Appleton-Century-Crofts, 1965), 4.
3. Erich W. Zimmerman, *World Resources and Industries* (New York: Harper, 1933), 3.
4. Charles E. Hinkson, *Traveler Profiles: A Study of Summer Travel in Alaska during 1963 and 1964* (Juneau: Dept of Economic Development and Planning, 1964), 6.

5. Jerome S. Bruner, "Personal Dynamics and the Process of Perceiving," in *Perception*, eds. Robert R. Blake and Glenn V. Ramsey (New York: The Ronald Press, 1951), 123.

6. Eugene Raskin, *Architecturally Speaking* (New York: Reinhold, 1954), 28.

7. Bruner, "Personal Dynamics," 126.

8. Kenneth E. Boulding, *The Image* (Ann Arbor, Michigan: The University of Michigan Press, 1956), 86.

9. Bruner, "Personal Dynamics," 126.

10. Ibid.

11. William N. Dember, *The Psychology of Perception* (New York: Holt, Rinehart & Winston, 1964), 273.

12. Samuel Howard Bartley, *Principles of Perception*, 2nd ed. (New York: Harper & Row, 1969).

13. John Steinbeck, *Travels with Charley* (New York: Viking, 1961), 149.

14. Henry James, *The Art of Travel: Scenes and Journeys in America, England, France, and Italy from the Travel Writings of Henry James*, ed. Morton Dauwen Zabel (Garden City, New York: Doubleday, 1958), 541.

15. John A. Howard and Jagdish N. Sheth, *The Theory of Buyer Behavior* (New York: Wiley, 1969).

16. Harold H. Kassarjian and Thomas S. Robertson, *Perspectives in Consumer Behavior* (Glenview, Illinois: Scott, Foresman, 1973), 8.

17. A. Parasuraman et al., "A Conceptual Model of Service Quality and Its Implications for Future Research" (monograph) (Cambridge, Massachusetts: Marketing Science Institute, 1984), 2.

18. Hal Norvell, "Outlook for Retired/Older Traveler Market Segments," proceedings, *1985–86 Outlook for Travel and Tourism* (Washington, D.C.: U.S. Travel Data Center, 1986), 125–44.

19. Charles D. Schewe and Roger J. Calantone, "Psychographic Segmentation of Tourists," *Journal of Travel Research* 16, no. 3 (Winter 1978): 14.

20. Edward Mayo, "Tourism and the National Parks: A Psychographic and Attitudinal Study," *Journal of Travel Research* 14, no. 1 (Summer 1975): 14.

21. Stanley C. Plog, "Conclusions from Two Decades of Travel Research," in *The Battle for Market Share: Strategies in Research and Marketing*, proceedings, 16th annual conference (Salt Lake City, Utah: The Travel and Tourism Research Association, 1985), 122.

22. Edward J. Mayo and Lance P. Jarvis, *The Psychology of Leisure Travel* (Boston: CBI Publishing, 1981), 194.

23. Arnold Mitchell, *The Nine American Lifestyles* (New York: Macmillan, 1983).

24. David Shih, "VALS as a Tool of Tourism Market Research: The Pennsylvania Experience," *Pennsylvania Travel Review* 6, no. 1 (January 1985): 6.

25. Daniel J. Stynes, "A Review and Evaluation of Market Segmentation Applications in Recreation and Tourism" (presentation at National Park and Recreation Association Symposium on Leisure Research, Dallas, 25–28 October 1985), 6.

26. Tom McMillan, *Tourism Tomorrow: Towards a Canadian Tourism Strategy* (Ottawa, Canada: Tourism Canada, 1985), 3.

27. Plog, "Conclusions," 128.

28. Douglas C. Frechtling, *U.S. Market for Package Tours* (Washington, D.C.: U.S. Travel Data Center, 1984), 6, 15.

29. Barbara E. Bryant and Andrew J. Morrison, "Travel Market Segmentation and the Implementation of Market Strategies," *Journal of Travel Research* 18, no. 3 (Winter 1980): 5.

30. Karen Cooke, "Guidelines for Socially Appropriate Tourism Development in British Columbia," *Journal of Travel Research* 21, no. 1 (Summer 1982): 22.

31. Lane L. Marshall, *Action by Design: Facilitating Design Decisions into the 21st Century* (Washington, D.C.: The American Society of Landscape Architects, 1983), 89.

32. Ibid., 95.

33. Lisa Germany, "Fair or Foul," *Texas Monthly* 114, no. 1 (January 1986): 254.

34. Clint Page and Penelope Cuff, eds., *Negotiating for Amenities, Part II* (Washington, D.C.: Partners for Livable Places, 1982).
35. Ibid., 27.
36. Ibid., 29.
37. Ibid., 40.
38. Wisconsin Department of Transportation, *Wisconsin's Rustic Roads* (leaflet) (Madison, Wisconsin: Wisconsin Department of Transportation, n.d.).
39. Lawrence Halprin, *The RSVP Cycles: Creative Processes in the Human Environment* (New York: George Braziller, 1969); Philip Thiel, "A Sequence-Experience Notation for Architectural and Urban Spaces," *Town Planning Review* 32, no. 1 (1961): 33–52; and Richard Pohlman, "A System for Recording Behavior and Occupying Design," in *Representation and Architecture* (Silver Spring, Maryland: Information Dynamics, 1982).
40. David Lowenthal, "The American Scene," in *Environmental Psychology*, eds. Harold M. Proshansky, William H. Ittelson, and Leanne G. Rivlin (New York: Holt, Rinehart & Winston, 1970), 295.

**Chapter 4. Attractions: First Power**
1. William Shakespeare, *The Two Gentlemen of Verona*, act 1, sc. 3.
2. Foster Rhea Dulles, *Americans Abroad: Two Centuries of European Travel* (Ann Arbor, Michigan: The University of Michigan Press, 1964), 29.
3. Frederick Jackson Turner, *The Frontier in American History* (New York: Henry Holt, 1920), 38.
4. Foster Rhea Dulles, *A History of Recreation: America Learns to Play*, 2nd ed., rev. (New York: Appleton-Century-Crofts, 1965): 6.
5. Ibid., 52.
6. Ibid., 396.
7. Alister Mathieson and Geoffrey Wall, *Tourism—Economic, Physical and Social Impacts* (London: Longman, 1982), 94.
8. Travel Industry Association of America, *Official Guidebook to Attractions America*, Resource Manual Membership Directory, National Council of Travel Attractions (Washington, D.C.: Travel Industry Association of America, 1983).
9. Paul Shepard, *Man in the Landscape* (New York: Knopf, 1967), 33.
10. Johnson, Johnson & Roy, Inc., *Marshall: A Plan for Preservation* (report) (Ann Arbor, Michigan: Johnson, Johnson & Roy, Inc., 1973), 2.
11. "Historical Townscapes in Britain: A Problem in Applied Geography," *The Urban Landscape: Historical Development and Management*, ed. J.W.R. Whitehand (New York: Academic Press, 1981), 58.
12. Mathieson and Wall, *Tourism*, 173.
13. Pierre Berton, "Foreword," *Reviving Main Street*, ed. Deryck Holdsworth (Toronto: University of Toronto Press, 1985), vii.

**Chapter 5. Tourism Destinations**
1. Alister Mathieson and Geoffrey Wall, *Tourism—Economic, Physical and Social Impacts* (London: Longman, 1982), 22.
2. Clare A. Gunn, "Destination Zone Fallacies and Half-Truths," *Tourism Management* 3, no. 4 (December 1982): 263–69.
3. Peter E. Murphy, *Tourism: A Community Approach* (New York: Methuen, 1985), 10.
4. Clare A. Gunn, *Mineral Wells: Opportunities for Tourism Development* (College Station, Texas: Texas A&M University System, Texas Agricultural Extension Service, 1985).
5. Clare A. Gunn, *Tourism Planning* 2nd ed. (New York: Taylor & Francis, 1988).

**Chapter 6. Design for a Purpose**
1. Wisconsin Department of Transportation, *Wisconsin's Rustic Roads* (leaflet) (Madison, Wisconsin: Wisconsin Department of Transportation, The Rustic Roads Board, n.d.).
2. Ronald Wiedenhoeft, "Walkable Cities: New Approaches to Environmental Management," *Proceedings of Sixth Annual Pedestrian Conference* (Boulder, Colorado, 19–20 September 1985), 22.
3. Sydney R. Fonnesbeck et al., "The Triad

Center: A Public-Private Partnership with an Emphasis on Human-Oriented Spaces," *Proceedings of Sixth Annual Pedestrian Conference* (Boulder, Colorado, 19–20 September 1985), 83.

4. Roy C. Buck and Ted Alleman, "Tourist Enterprise Concentration and Old Order Amish Survival: Explorations in Productive Coexistence," *Journal of Travel Research* 18, no. 1 (Summer 1979): 15–20.

5. Joe Digles, "City in Orbit," *Nevada Magazine* 41, no. 2 (March–April 1981): 53.

6. National and Historic Parks Branch Indian Affairs and Northern Development, *National Parks Policy* (Ottawa, Canada: The Queen's Printer, 1969), 4.

7. Richard R. Forster, *Planning for Men and Nature in National Parks* (Morges, Switzerland: International Union for Conservation of Nature and Natural Resources, 1973), 49.

8. B. K. Downie, "Reflections on the National Park Zoning System," *The Operational Geographer* 3 (1984): 15.

9. Clare A. Gunn, "Resource Management for Visitors," *Fish and Wildlife News* (October–November 1979): 20.

10. Joseph L. Sax, *Mountains Without Handrails* (Ann Arbor, Michigan: The University of Michigan Press, 1980), 111.

11. Ibid., 103.

12. Carl O. Sauer, "Seashore—Primitive Home of Man?" in *Land and Life*, ed. John Leighly (Berkeley, California: University of California Press, 1967), 310.

13. Clare A. Gunn, "Concentrated Dispersal, Dispersed Concentration—A Pattern for Saving Scarce Coastlines," *Landscape Architecture* 62, no. 2 (1972): 133.

14. Clare A. Gunn et al., *Development of Criteria for Evaluating Urban River Settings for Tourism-Recreation Use*, Bulletin MP-1139, Texas Agricultural Experiment Station (College Station, Texas: Texas Water Resources Institute, 1974), 61–69. (Diagrams L, M, N, O by Marmon, Mok, and Green, Inc., landscape architects.)

15. American Society of Landscape Architects Foundation and U.S. Department of Housing and Urban Development, *Barrier Free Site Design* (Washington, D.C.: U.S. Government Printing Office, 1977): 20.

16. Romedi Passini, *Wayfinding in Architecture* (New York: Van Nostrand Reinhold, 1984), 165.

17. Ibid., 46.

## Chapter 7. Design Principles

1. Garrett Ekbo, "The Landscape of Tourism," *Landscape* 18, no. 2 (Spring–Summer 1969), 31.

2. Omer Akin and Eleanor F. Weinel, eds., *Representation and Architecture* (Silver Spring, Maryland: Information Dynamics, 1982), 93.

3. John Ormsbee Simonds, *Landscape Architecture*, 2nd ed. (New York: McGraw-Hill, 1983); and Norman K. Booth, *Basic Elements of Landscape Architectural Design* (New York: Elsevier, 1985).

4. Forrest Wilson, *A Graphic Survey of Perception and Behavior for the Design Professions* (New York: Van Nostrand Reinhold, 1984), 3.

5. Henry Vincent Hubbard and Theodora Kimball, *An Introduction to the Study of Landscape Design*, rev. ed. (New York: Macmillan, 1929), 89.

6. Simonds, *Landscape Architecture*, 19.

7. Ibid., 111.

8. Ibid., 207.

9. George R. Stewart, *Names on the Land* (Boston: Houghton Mifflin, 1967), 91.

10. Gyorgy Kepes, *The New Landscape in Art and Science* (Chicago: Paul Theobald, 1956).

11. Booth, *Basic Elements*, 130.

12. Ibid., 107.

13. Alan Chimacoff, "Figure, System and Memory: The Process of Design," in *Representation and Architecture*, eds. Omer Akin and Eleanor F. Weinel (Silver Spring, Maryland: Information Dynamics, 1982), 146.

14. Wolfgang M. Zucker, "The Image and Imagination of the Architect," in *Via 6, Architecture and Visual Perception*, eds.

Alice Gray Read and Peter C. Doo (Cambridge, Massachusetts: MIT Press, 1983), 22.

15. Clarence J. Glacken, "Reflections on the Man-Nature Theme as a Subject for Study," in *Future Environments of North America*, eds. F. Fraser Darling and John P. Milton (Garden City, New York: The Natural History Press, 1966), 368.

## Chapter 8. Design Techniques

1. Charles M. Eastman, "The Computer as a Design Medium," in *Representation and Architecture*, eds. Omer Akin and Eleanor F. Weinel (Silver Spring, Maryland: Information Dynamics, 1982), 148.

2. Meir Gross and Julie DelVecchio Smith, "Artificial Intelligence: A New Frontier in Landscape Planning," *Regional Landscape Planning* (Washington, D.C.: American Society of Landscape Architects, 1984), 47.

3. Ibid., 43.

4. Kathy L. Wolf, "Computer-Aided Design: An Interview with Professor William Johnson," *Michiganscapes* (Spring 1985): 3.

5. Charles Killpack and S. J. Camarata, "The Role of Micro-Computers in Environmental Site Assessment," *Regional Landscape Planning* (Washington, D.C.: American Society of Landscape Architects, 1983), 16.

6. Division of Recreation and Cultural Resources, Bureau of Land Management, *Visual Simulation Techniques* (Washington, D.C.: U.S. Government Printing Office, 1980), 5.

7. Gary Elsner and Robert Ross, Jr., "Real Computers for Real Landscape Architects," *Regional Landscape Planning* (Washington, D.C.: American Society of Landscape Architects, 1984), 4.

8. Robert W. Ross, Jr., "The Development and Adaptation of Computer Applications for Landscape Planning and Management on National Forest System Lands in the United States," (unpublished paper) (Washington, D.C.: USDA Forest Service, 1986).

9. Charles Killpack, "Landsat: Innovative Landscape Architecture," *LATIS*, Landscape Architecture Technical Information, Series 6 (Washington, D.C.: American Society of Landscape Architects, 1982), 20.

10. David M. Oliver and Valdis D. Zusmanis, "The Impact of Operational Satellite Systems," *Regional Landscape Planning* (Washington, D.C.: American Society of Landscape Architects, 1984), 25.

11. Brian Orland, "Image Advantage," *Landscape Architecture* 76, no. 1 (Jan.–Feb. 1986): 58.

12. David W. Goldberg, "Computer Based Videographics" (Master's thesis, Department of Architecture, Texas A&M University, June 1986), 53–95.

13. Robert C. Maggio and Douglas F. Wunneburger, "A Microcomputer-based Geographic Information System for Natural Resource Managers" (unpublished paper, Department of Forest Science, Texas A&M University, 1986).

14. Jean Meadows, ed., *A Manager's Guide to Geographic Information Systems*, Natural Resources Report Series 86-1, rev. (Atlanta, Georgia: National Park Service, June 1986).

15. Clare A. Gunn, *Tourism Development: Assessment of Potential in Texas*, Bulletin MP-1416 (College Station, Texas: Texas A&M University System, Texas Agricultural Experiment Station, 1979); and Clare A. Gunn, *Tourism Planning* (New York: Crane Russak, 1979).

16. Ontario Hydro, *Southwestern Ontario Transmission Study, Environmental Assessment, Volume 2* (Bruce Nuclear Power Development to Essa Transformer Station Route Selection) (Toronto: Ontario Hydro, 1985).

## Chapter 9. Gallery of Well-Designed Places

1. Joel A. Glass, "Designing Hotels on a Human Scale," *Hotel & Resort Industry* 8, no. 11 (November 1985): 18.

2. "Waterfront Park," (Merit Award, Professional Awards Program, ASLA), *Land-*

*scape Architecture* 71, no. 5 (September 1981): 612.

3. "Oregon Dunes Overlook," (Merit Award, Professional Awards Program, ASLA), *Landscape Architecture* 74, no. 5 (September/October 1984): 79.

4. "Fiddler's Green Amphitheatre," (Honor Design, Professional Awards Program, ASLA), *Landscape Architecture* 74, no. 5 (September/October 1984): 66.

**Chapter 10. Epilogue**

1. John Allen et al., *The Foundations of Free Enterprise* (Economic Education Series, no. 1) (College Station, Texas: Texas A&M University, Center for Education and Research in Free Enterprise, 1979).

2. Clare A. Gunn, "Small Town and Rural Tourism Planning" (presentation, conference on Integrated Development Beyond the City, Mt. Allison University, Sackville, New Brunswick, 14 June 1986).

3. G. Wall, "The Nature of Outdoor Recreation," in *Recreation Land Use in Southern Ontario*, ed. G. Wall (Waterloo: University of Waterloo, 1979), 3–13.

4. William Least Heat Moon, *Blue Highways: A Journey into America* (Boston: Little, Brown, 1982).

5 Reg Lang, "Integration: What It Means to Planners" (presentation, conference on Integrated Development Beyond the City, Mt. Allison University, Sackville New Brunswick, 11 June 1986), 12.

# Index